Smart Talk

What Kids Say About Growing Up Gifted

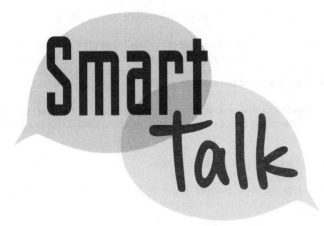

What Kids Say About
Growing Up Gifted

Robert A. Schultz, Ph.D.
James R. Delisle, Ph.D.

Illustrated by Tyler Page

free spirit
PUBLiSHiNG®

Helping kids
help themselves™
since 1983

Library of Congress Cataloging-in-Publication Data
Schultz, Robert A., 1942–
    Smart talk : what kids say about growing up gifted / Robert A. Schultz and James R. Delisle.
      p. cm.
    Includes index.
    ISBN-13: 978-1-57542-205-3
    ISBN-10: 1-57542-205-0
    1. Gifted children—Education—United States. 2. Gifted children—United States—Attitudes.
I. Delisle, James R., 1953– II. Title.
    LC3993.9.S387 2006
    371.95—dc22

                                                                                    2006017915

At the time of this book's publication, all facts and figures cited are the most current available. All telephone numbers, addresses, and Web site URLs are accurate and active; all publications, organizations, Web sites, and other resources exist as described in this book; and all have been verified as of May 2006. The authors and Free Spirit Publishing make no warranty or guarantee concerning the information and materials given out by organizations or content found at Web sites, and we are not responsible for any changes that occur after this book's publication. If you find an error or believe that a resource listed here is not as described, please contact Free Spirit Publishing. Parents, teachers, and other adults: We strongly urge you to monitor children's use of the Internet.

Edited by Eric Braun
Cover and interior design by Marti Naughton

10 9 8 7 6 5 4 3 2 1
Printed in the United States of America

Free Spirit Publishing Inc.
217 Fifth Avenue North, Suite 200
Minneapolis, MN 55401-1299
(612) 338-2068
help4kids@freespirit.com
www.freespirit.com

Printed on recycled paper
including 30%
post-consumer waste

green press
INITIATIVE

Dedication

There is a time when one realizes life is meaningless without another.
That time came for me May 20, 1989—then history repeated itself
March 2, 1998, and again May 31, 2000. All I am belongs to Cindy,
Brendon, and Caytlin. Your lessons teach me every day what
it means to be and become. This book is dedicated to you.
—R.A.S.

This book also is dedicated to Annemarie Roeper, my "gifted
grandmother." More than any other individual, you have shown me
the importance of listening to children. Thank you for every
lesson you have ever taught me, Annemarie.
—J.R.D.

Acknowledgments

Thank you to the more than 4,000 gifted kids from around the world who took the time to share their thoughts and feelings and lay the foundation for this book. Thanks especially to the "A Kid Like You" contributors who painted even more colorful canvasses of their lives as gifted kids. A hearty thanks goes to Eric Braun, our editor, who helped carve a manuscript that sings out of an encyclopedic compendium of many, many, many stories. And finally, to our families: thank you for your support, input, and sacrifices as this book came together.

Contents

5 Home: Life with Family 75

Introduction

Being gifted is being different. Maybe you learned to read earlier than most kids your age. Maybe you use and understand vocabulary well beyond your grade level or constantly have to explain your fascination with topics (like limnology!) that others think are strange. Or maybe you just don't seem to be interested in the same things as other kids your age. Whatever the reasons are, the result is the same: you're different.

Being different does have its upsides. Some of the things gifted kids say they like about being gifted are:

- Schoolwork is usually pretty easy, and you finish homework quickly.
- You get treated like an adult sometimes.
- You can help your friends with schoolwork if they're stuck, and some kids look up to you.

But for many gifted kids, being different is a burden. You might get teased for being smart, some students might ask you for help or answers a lot, and school can be boring. Your parents might have really high expectations of you, and it can be hard to make and keep friends. On top of that, a lot of gifted kids feel like it's their fault they're so different. (It's not.)

As professors in gifted education, teachers of gifted students, parents of gifted kids, and gifted individuals ourselves, we've learned that being gifted is more than what you are able to do. It's a big part of *who you are.* We've worked with many people over the years who thought they, their kids, or their friends were weird because they were gifted. This book will show you that they—and you—are not. Within the covers of this book, hundreds of gifted kids just like you share their experiences. You can feel connected with others who share similar life experiences: kids who learn at a quick pace, have topics they're passionate about, feel frustrated in school, have a difficult time making new friends, or get completely lost within the imaginative worlds of their minds.

How This Book Came to Be

A lot of people have completed piles of research projects and studies to try to understand giftedness. But we believe the most important understanding comes from the people whose voices are least likely to be heard in research reports—gifted individuals themselves.

So in 2003 we began asking gifted young people to tell us about themselves. We posted a survey at our Web site, www.giftedkidspeak.com, asking what they like and what they don't like about being gifted.

> Most of the responses came from kids in the United States and Canada, but we also heard from Russia, the Netherlands, Germany, China, Japan, Uzbekistan, Philippines, Great Britain, Australia, and many more.

We asked them to share thoughts about their peers, their families, their schooling, and the future.

And share they did! Thousands of kids and teens responded to our survey. For this book we collected some of the most common answers, as well as some of the most interesting and funny ones, from kids 4 to 12 years old.

We also gathered more in-depth personal stories about gifted kids. These biographies, called "A Kid Like You," are sprinkled throughout the book and give you an even deeper look into the minds and lives of other gifted kids.

How to Use This Book

How you read this book is up to you. You can read it straight through. You can jump around to chapters or questions that reflect issues that are important to you. Or you can just read responses from other kids your age (responses to each question are listed from youngest to oldest). Check out the Contents to see all the questions and where to find them.

As you read the questions and responses, think about how *you* would answer the questions. If you feel like it, jot down your responses in a journal, on a piece of scratch paper, or on a computer. Throughout the book you'll also find "Reflection/Connection" boxes that can help you explore more deeply the issues raised by the questions.

Finally, think about the responses and how they compare to your own thoughts and experiences. Which responses make sense to you? Which ones don't sound right? Are there any ideas you never thought of before?

We hope you learn as much about giftedness (and yourself) from reading *Smart Talk* as we did from putting it together. Think of this book as the beginning of the discussion. What's missing is what *you* have to say about giftedness. After reading, if you decide you have something to add, we want to hear from you! Send your story to us at the address below or visit our survey at www.giftedkidspeak.com. Even if you don't want to participate in the survey, we'd love to hear how you liked this book. You can write or email us at:

Bob Schultz and Jim Delisle
Free Spirit Publishing
217 Fifth Avenue North, Suite 200
Minneapolis, MN 55401-1299
help4kids@freespirit.com

We look forward to hearing from you!

Giftedness:
What's It Mean to You?

What does it mean when you get labeled "gifted"? Is it something you'll outgrow? Can you be cured? Will you ever be the same again?

As with most labels, people have a lot of assumptions, perceptions, and misconceptions about giftedness. If you don't believe us, ask any three people how they define giftedness. We bet you'll get three completely different answers.

Here's one thing we know about the gifted *label*: it doesn't change who you are. Labels are just tools to help us understand and communicate what things mean in our lives. In this chapter, we look at what many gifted kids think of themselves and their label.

What do you think being gifted means? What is your reaction to the term GIFTED?

To me, being gifted means I am talented above the norm. Most people don't compose symphonies or need to play the piano the way I do. They seem to like a lot of boring things and don't understand half of what I talk about.
Girl, 8, New Mexico

I think it means being different from other people and you have your own special talent. Sometimes you can be a little bit weird.
Girl, 9, Oregon

I'm just a kid just a little out of the ordinary. I don't look at myself as a rocket scientist or a genius.
Boy, 10, Illinois

To me, the word gifted is a relatively benign label for the academically and/or artistically profound students in any subject area. I do not feel any great opposition to the term, as it is merely psychological jargon used to define a certain classification of cognitive functioning, but when it comes to such specific words as "profoundly" or "moderately" gifted, I grow frustrated. For example, a child with a very constricted gift may feel inferior to a globally gifted child with the same label.
Boy, 10, Massachusetts

I think being gifted means being able to do things other people can't, and doing better in school than others. When I heard that I was gifted, I was very surprised because I thought I was just like other kids and not very different.
Girl, 10, Wisconsin

I think being gifted means that I have a special way of expressing myself that others don't have.
Girl, 10, Ohio

I think gifted is another term for a different mind; a significant mind.
Boy, 11, Ontario, Canada

I think being gifted not only means to be smarter than an average
person of your age group, but that we have a different perspective
of things a normal person would just overlook. A gifted person has a
much easier time understanding things around them, and because of
that they go much faster and have
the time to search every nook and
cranny of a problem.
Boy, 11, Kentucky

> "I'm just a kid just a little out of the ordinary."

I believe that being gifted
means that your hydrangea has
blossomed earlier than that of others,
not meaning that we all have the same
gifts. I react to the term gifted like I react to pineapple: good, but with
some drawbacks, like when you don't know an answer or when you
have to ask for help, and the other kids look at you funny and say,
"You're supposed to be a genius," or "HE had to ask ME for help?"
Boy, 11, Wisconsin

I think it means to have the ability to do more. I ALWAYS add detail!
Girl, 11, Indiana

I think gifted means that you are able to understand more complex
problems and that you are enriched in critical thinking skills.
Boy, 12, Ohio

I think being gifted means that you are more advanced in a certain
subject or activity. Hearing this makes me happy and upset at the same
time. When I am labeled gifted, I feel like I have to be perfect or all of
my friends will think that there is something wrong with me.
Girl, 12, New York

Reflection Connection

What do you think being gifted means?

Come up with your own definition of *gifted,* then become an investigative reporter. Ask friends, parents, teachers, cousins, and anyone else you like for their definition. Ask gifted people and people who haven't been labeled gifted. Next, find out if your school has a formal definition of giftedness, and if so, write that down (or get a copy). Finally, compare all these answers. What do they have in common? How are they different? Which definition is best? Why?

How are you the same as and different from other children your age?

A lot of children like to play. I do not. My favorite thing to do is to read to my imaginary horses. When I finish a book, I like to discuss with them and have their opinion on the book. We don't judge each other.
Girl, 6, Florida

I'm different. Let's leave it at that. I'm just different.
Boy, 7, Ohio

I am pretty much the same as other boys. I like many of the same things, like dinosaurs, baseball, and swimming (who doesn't like these things?). I am different in these ways: I do highly advanced math for my age. I like origami a lot.
Boy, 7, California

The only thing I noticed is that there are a lot of things I think of about life that most children my age don't. But sometimes I wish I didn't think as much.
Girl, 7, Montana

I like being quiet. I like time to myself a lot too. I like to think. Sometimes my thoughts take me to really strange places inside my head and that's fun.
Girl, 8, New Mexico

I understand things other kids don't. I have advanced humor. I'm not as goofy and I'm more serious. I "get" things other kids don't understand when it comes to humor/jokes.
Girl, 9, Illinois

I find myself different in every category. If the teacher says only one person aced a test, everyone assumes I got it.
Boy, 10, Ohio

I have the same interests as other kids, I make friends, I act like a regular kid, I am not a weird creature from outer space!
Girl, 10, Nevada

I have never been taken with sports, and I have read books that many people have only seen in the adult fiction section of the library. I am a published author, and I happen to sometimes know more on a subject than my teachers.
Boy, 11, Wisconsin

I have very bad social relationships— I fight tooth and nail to AVOID going to the mall, and I think crocodiles and anacondas are cute. These are not qualities that you would usually find in a regular sixth grade environment. I have pretty good memorization skills; I know the first seventy-one decimal places of pi and the first sixty-eight elements of the periodic table.
Girl, 11, Nebraska

According to my teacher, I am different in my odd learning way. I learn faster and sometimes I get a bit frustrated having to show work when clear answers come to my head.
Boy, 11, Texas

I think my maturity level is the same, mostly. I cry more easily and I get more upset over things and speak before I think, but then again I'm a lot more independent and self-sufficient. So less mature in some ways—interpersonal—and more mature in intrapersonal stuff.
Girl, 12, Nebraska

I am the same as other children my age because I laugh at dumb jokes and can have a lot of fun. I am different because I have interests that no one my age cares about. I am really into philosophy, self-improvement, and taking care of my body.
Girl, 12, Ohio

How did you find out that you are gifted?

My sister told me that I was gifted. I did not know what it meant so she explained it to me that I was different from other kids but that was okay. I had just accepted that regular children prefer to play Barbie than to read and that when I was feeling lonely, I would just have to imitate them.
Girl, 6, Florida

From the leprechaun under my bed.
Boy, 7, Ohio

I thought everybody could play piano like me until I started school. The other kids didn't even know how to read. I can't remember a time when I couldn't read or play piano or write poetry. Most of the others didn't even know what poetry was.
Girl, 8, New Mexico

I learned from the standardized tests given in spring at school. Also because I was getting in trouble in class for being bored.
Girl, 8, Ohio

I found out in kindergarten, when we were making Indian costumes for a pow-wow and learning about Indians. Everyone else just did a blob of feathers and beads and stuck it on, but I thought it was fun to do interesting patterns. That was when I knew.
Girl, 9, Florida

A school psychologist from outside my school district told me because she knew I was feeling frustrated about my inability to physically write.
Boy, 10, Illinois

I found out I was gifted by mail. Someone asked me (in the mail) if I wanted to come to enrichment.
Girl, 10, Ohio

I took a test that was weird and I guess I passed.
Boy, 10, Texas

My doctor told my mom I was gifted when I was born.
Boy, 11, New York

I told my mom in kindergarten there were no numbers smaller than zero (that's what the teacher told us) and she drew a number line showing me negative numbers. Well, I started adding and subtracting them. I also asked her what multiplication meant and she said, "It is just adding in sets of . . ." I got it. All of it just made sense. My mom had me tested in first grade and they said yes, I was gifted, then pretty much ignored me.
Girl, 11, Ohio

To make a long story short, I was in second grade, happy as could be. My parents told me I had been accepted into the program. Then, suddenly, I was different than everyone else.
Boy, 11, Ohio

I think I realized I was gifted when my second grade teacher would get furious if I pointed out that she was wrong—I assumed everyone wanted to know when they made a mistake because I always (usually) want to know.
Girl, 11, Texas

I took a cute little test and it came back genius.
Girl, 12, Ohio

Tests, grades, comments, lots of things. It's not like someone came up to me and said, "Hey kid! You're gifted!"
Girl, 12, Ohio

Reflection Connection

How did you find out you are gifted? Did you suspect you were gifted (or different) before you were actually labeled or identified? What, if anything, changed once you were identified?

Do you enjoy being gifted? Explain.

Yes, no, maybe so. I like to be a little different, but sometimes I feel out of place with my friends and surroundings.
Boy, 9, Ohio

Yes, I think going to the high school to take classes helps me to be more responsible. I also learn how to avoid big high schoolers' feet so I don't get stepped on.
Boy, 9, Idaho

So-so. Some people look up to me, but some people think I'm a freak.
Boy, 11, Japan

I enjoy being gifted because we do fun activities and I'm being challenged more, unlike last year when I wasn't challenged much.
Girl, 11, Ohio

I know it may sound odd or mean, but I enjoy having my friends questioning me and giving them answers that lead to more questions.
Boy, 11, New York

I don't enjoy it because people who might be jealous of me call me "the nerd" or "the brainiac" or "teacher's pet" (because my teacher loves to recognize me in front of class). And my friends think that because I am gifted, I know everything, so they'll ask me a question I might not be able to answer, and then they say, "I thought you knew everything."
Boy, 11, New Hampshire

It helps in life to have a mind that can help you solve your problems and get you out of sticky situations. Plus, I always wanted to be a little famous. Since I'm gifted, I feel that I stand out a little bit and have a lot of interesting opportunities ahead.
Girl, 12, Ohio

A Kid Like You: Evan, Age 12

Evan lives in a suburb of Boston, Massachusetts, with his mom, dad, and two cats that he describes as "wonderfully furry beings who wreak havoc daily." The cats, Cassie and Hubble, are named after the famous astronomers Giovanni Cassini and Edwin Hubble. Evan says, "Our family is extremely quirky, so there are many ways to be strange, odd, or weird, any day of the week."

Gifted kids often say they feel like they're weird, or not normal. Living in a family that values weirdness probably has made growing up gifted easier for Evan than for a lot of kids. "In my opinion, being gifted is exactly the same as being an average person," he says, "except you can experience things and do things with so much more passion than one might expect. Giftedness

→

I will also describe as natural ability, but this skill or state of being is usually fueled with passion."

What are some of the things Evan is passionate about? Here's what he says:

- Drumming: I sometimes perform and have weekly lessons.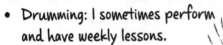
- Drawing: Right now I'm doing a lot of fashion design, manga, lettering, and figure drawing. I also enjoy abstract and contour.
- Writing: I write all different kinds of stuff: fan fiction, journalism, poetry, historical fiction, nonfiction, html, and loads of others.
- Origami: It used to take up my whole life.
- Reading: I am absolutely obsessed with Harry Potter, Artemis Fowl, J.R.R. Tolkien, and most other fantasy.
- Drama: I love it! This activity makes me feel so free and happy and makes me forget anything that may be on my mind!
- Photography: I'm thinking of entering a contest to see if the passion I have is recognized by others.

Though many kids say they suspected they were gifted—or different—before they were actually labeled, Evan did not. Before he was tested, the year he turned 5, he says, "I had just been doing things that I considered normal. It wasn't like I had this awesome power locked up inside me that could save the world or something like that. Just a normal kid in a normal house, with normal parents and normal friends.

"Now, it's different," he continues. "I know all the labels, the good and the bad, I know why I qualify for lots of things, but I hope that I'm not judged from them. In the end, we're all just people, aren't we?"

What are the most and least important things to you about being gifted?

The most important thing about being gifted is I get to beat everyone in my family in arguments. The least important thing about being gifted is all the extra homework.

Boy, 7, Kentucky

The most important things are that I get to work ahead and I get to feel special, which is fun. The least important thing is I get called "smart" and "gifted" by some people.

Girl, 9, Pennsylvania

The most important thing about me being gifted is that I get challenged when I need it. The least important thing about being gifted is that "I know everything," and kids are always asking me what the square root of so and so is. I just want to fit in and be normal, but it's hard when you stick out like a lollipop in a pile of jelly beans.

Boy, 9, Ohio

The most important thing to me is that I am in a class where I am challenged to a higher standard.

Boy, 10, New York

The most important thing to me about being gifted is to respect other kids who aren't gifted and to do my best. The least important thing to me about being gifted is to show off to other kids and rub it in their faces that I'm smarter than them. I never do that to anyone because it is CRUEL.

Girl, 11, Indiana

Do you ever wish you were NOT gifted? Explain.

Whenever I'm pestered and pushed around, then I wish I was like everyone else.
Boy, 7, Ohio

Sometimes, because I get lots of extra homework, but I think that it will pay off because I will get into a good college and graduate to be a teacher or author or pediatrician. I just want to be normal, and fit in with the kids all around me.
Boy, 9, Idaho

No, I never wish that I was not gifted because it is a good thing to have an assignment that is a challenge.
Girl, 9, Ohio

I like knowing that I'm special and talented. It gives me a glowing feeling that I wouldn't trade for the world!
Boy, 10, Ohio

It's hard to be gifted. I have to do things by myself. There isn't really anybody I know when I take special classes, and even though I make friends it's hard to be away from the people I know really well.
Girl, 10, Pennsylvania

Yes, because my parents expect me to be so smart, and I can't do funny things with my friends.
Boy, 11, West Virginia

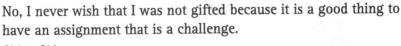
"I just want to be normal."

Yes, because I do not think I would be pressured as much by my parents and there would not be as much expected from me.
Girl, 11, North Carolina

Reflection Connection

"Gifted" and "Talented."

Using one or both of those words, make an acrostic poem sharing who you are or how you feel about being gifted. A couple examples follow. If you prefer, come up with your own theme words to build a poem around.

Growing as
I learn to
Fit into
Teams where just playing is important.
Each time I
Do this makes me feel good.

I want to know all the rules before I play; but, I'm getting better at just playing. This is gifted to me. —Boy, 8, Montana

in **T**ense
Active
Lonely
Energized
Not many friends
Thinker
Even tempered
Demanding

That's me to a tee! —Girl, 11, Iowa

What are the best and worst things about being gifted?

The best thing is that people can end up being really proud of you for accomplishing something. The worst thing about being gifted is that people can really put you down just talking to you. Older kids say "you're too young to do that" or "you're too small to do that" or "you're too small to be that active."

Girl, 6, Arizona

I got to join chess club in kindergarten, but usually you have to wait until third grade.

Boy, 6, Texas

The best thing about being gifted is I don't have to go to school. Instead I get to spend tons of time with my dad. We follow the stock market together and restore his airplane. We spend tons of time working on my tanks and researching sea life. The worst part of being gifted is that some people act like I have to do this or that because somehow I owe somebody for my giftedness.

Girl, 8, New Mexico

Best: Sometimes people (adults) understand you better and you get treated with more respect. Worst: When adults treat you like a little kid and think you won't understand something. They don't think you can be involved in adult conversation.

Boy, 9, Illinois

The worst is getting in trouble for not completing work I miss when I go to my gifted class and then come back to my regular class the next day.

Girl, 10, Ohio

Best: Going to college is neat. Being gifted opens up doors to camps and a lot of fun learning. Worst: When I go to college some people look at me like I am weird, and of course my calculus class takes some work.

Girl, 10, Florida

The best is I feel GREAT about myself! The worst is that I feel separated sometimes.
Girl, 11, Ohio

The worst thing is that you get mind-numbingly BORED.
Girl, 11, West Virginia

Feeling different, but wanting to be the same. And sometimes, being the same, but wanting to remain different.
Boy, 11, North Carolina

The best thing is that your life feels so much richer with all of the thoughts you think and all the wonderful things you can do and learn that most people will never know. The worst thing is that there are not a lot of people you can relate to on an intellectual level and you feel so alone.
Girl, 12, Arizona

The best part about being gifted is I am being recognized. The worst part is when some find out you are gifted they feel they can get answers off of you.
Boy, 12, Nebraska

I feel really conflicted a lot of the time. Really confused. It feels like the more you understand, the more questions come up. I have soooooo many questions. I don't think some of them can really be answered. And I'm stuck in a little room memorizing stupid things (and reading a novel if the teacher is nice).
Girl, 12, Oregon

The worst thing about being gifted is that if something goes wrong it's always your fault because you should have known better.
Girl, 12, New York

Fitting In:
Friends and Peers

Lots of people struggle with fitting in, but for gifted kids the struggle is even more common. Some kids might tease or bully you, others might be your friend to get help on schoolwork, and others might just treat you *differently* somehow—when all you want is to be one of the gang.

For some, being different isn't a big deal. They are independent and confident. They like being gifted. Others find giftedness a burden. These kids may wrestle daily with the powerful need to fit in. They ask themselves questions like: *Should I stop answering questions in class so*

19

others won't notice me? Should I purposely get answers wrong so I'm not the one with the 100 again? Should I stop using all those big words?

A lot of gifted kids choose to have only a few close friends rather than many less-intense relationships. These close friendships—especially with other gifted kids—can be very rewarding. But friendships with nongifted peers also can be rewarding, so don't limit your social life to only gifted kids.

How do friends react to your abilities? What do friends do or say that makes you feel good or bad about being gifted?

Friends tend to be jealous and label me the "smart" kid. I get accused of bragging when I simply answer a question correctly.
Girl, 7, Washington

I feel good when they say, "Wow, that's really neat. I wish I had the abilities to do these things too." But sometimes they make me feel bad. They say it is just because I practiced a lot and that it doesn't have anything to do with being gifted and I am just making it up.
Boy, 9, Florida

I get really mad at my friends when they say things like the GT program is for "Smart-o-matics." That really hurts my feelings.
Girl, 10, Nebraska

My classmates make me feel bad because they ask me questions until I get something wrong. Then they say something humiliating about me being smart. I can't wait until eighth grade when I am not in the GT program anymore. Then they can't tease me anymore about being smart.
Boy, 10, Iowa

My friends react kind of surly toward me being gifted sometimes. One of them says I brag about it all the time and then imitates me. (Let's just say she's really mean about it.)
Girl, 10, Idaho

Sometimes they're sardonic, but most of my friends are like me.

Girl, 10, Kentucky

Kids hassle me about being young and in sixth grade (I skipped one grade).

Boy, 11, California

"A few people call me walking dictionary."

No one says anything except if my teacher says someone got over 100 percent. Everyone then says my name and looks at me, even if it isn't me!

Boy, 11, Texas

I heard rumors from some classmates that one boy is my "friend" so I can get good grades for him.

Girl, 11, Pennsylvania

Most of my friends think it's a good thing. A few people call me walking dictionary, though.

Boy, 11, New York

The students just are jealous of me and of my being allowed to go to Excel instead of going to regular class.

Boy, 11, Ohio

Friends? A few. All of them are gifted. What I like about the kids I tend to hang with is their unique senses of humor—I really enjoy gross topics. What I cannot stand about even some gifted kids is how ridiculously competitive they are—how they think that going for the throat to serve themselves is normal.

Girl, 11, Texas

They say you are so lucky that you get to be in GT because you get to go out of class for the day! I say to them that it is not all fun and games in the GT program. Last week we took a very long brain test over everything. It was very hard and it took me forever to study for it.

Girl, 11, Texas

Everybody thinks I'm just a goody-two-shoes, and I'm not. Just because I don't get in trouble as much as everybody else they think of me different, and it doesn't exactly make me feel confident about myself.
Boy, 12, Louisiana

Most of my friends aren't necessarily gifted, but they are smart. One of my friends has a program worked out with her language arts teacher so that she can have harder spelling words. I think my friends mostly agree with me when I say that math moves too slow. The only thing they act jealous about is my string bass playing abilities.
Girl, 12, Wisconsin

My friends respect it that I'm gifted. They know that I can't help it so they don't make fun of it. I just want one friend who doesn't care if I am smart or not—who doesn't want to be my class partner to get answers off me.
Girl, 12, Alaska

Reflection Connection

It's not uncommon for gifted kids to have just a few friends (even just one!), but these friendships tend to be deep—especially when intellectual peers find one another. That doesn't mean you can't have many casual friends, or nongifted friends. You can. But many gifted kids are happiest with a few intense friendships with other gifted kids who have the same interests or talents as them.

Of course, finding other gifted kids—especially ones who are into what you're into—can be hard. Giftedness is rare, after all. If you haven't found an intellectual peer in your local area, you may want to broaden your search. Get involved in activities that bring together kids from other locations. These activities give you more chances to connect.

$\longrightarrow$

Here are a few ideas. Can you think of others to add to the list?

1. Take online courses that interest you.
2. Join a club.
3. Go to a gifted conference where you can learn about (and meet) other gifted people.
4. Watch the local newspaper for events that interest you, such as lectures, concerts, and presentations (perhaps at a local school or college), and attend some.
5. Get involved with a charity or community service project that interests you.

How would you deal with seeing another gifted person being picked on?

I would definitely stand up for the gifted person because I hate getting picked on myself and if I stood up for that person they might become my friend and I would love to have a person like that as one of my friends.

Boy, 10, Oklahoma

I would step in and request that they leave that person alone. If not, I would go to a principal, teacher, or parent for help. This happened once and I stayed close to the victim who then became one of my best friends.

Girl, 11, New York

I really feel bad and try the best I can to help them because I know how it feels to be picked on because you're smart or weird.

Boy, 12, Florida

In my school gifted people don't get picked on really. I'd probably stand up for that person. It would make me feel a little bad.
Girl, 12, Pennsylvania

No One Deserves to Be Bullied

Bullying is when someone tries to hurt someone physically or with words. Bullying includes threats, put-downs, mean teasing, gossip, and pushing, kicking, or hitting. If any of these are happening to you, you can do something to stop it. Tell the person you want him or her to stop. Stand up straight, look the person in the eye, and speak clearly and firmly. You can say, "I don't like that and I want you to stop," or something more simple, like "Knock it off." If that doesn't work, get help from an adult such as a parent, teacher, or principal. This is *not* tattling. It is making sure you and your friends are safe. No one deserves to be bullied. For more tips on dealing with bullies, including making yourself bully-proof, check out *Bullies Are a Pain in the Brain* by Trevor Romain (Free Spirit Publishing, 1997).

A Kid Like You: Kelsey, Age 12

Making friends and fitting in are hard enough, but when you're the new kid in town it can be even harder. Twelve-year-old Kelsey has played the role of New Kid a lot. That's because her dad is in the Marines, and her family has moved often.

"I've lived in eight different places and been to three different schools," says Kelsey, who currently lives in a suburb of Toledo, Ohio. "I love where I live now."

Besides being new each time she moved, Kelsey also felt different from other kids because she was gifted. "First grade was when I realized I was different," she says. "I had a fourth-grade reading level and was put into Horizons (gifted classes). I didn't

→

see it as a big deal, really, but was proud." Other kids didn't single her out, and she didn't have trouble fitting in.

Later, things began to change.

"Sixth grade is when I've stood out the most. There is another kid in my class who also is gifted, and every day we get remarks like, 'You're smarter than me,' and 'I want to be on Kelsey or Dante's team so we can win!' Little things like that bother me because I don't want to stand out because of my ability to learn. I want people to get to know the real me, not judge what they see on the outside."

That can be a lot to expect from other kids when it looks to them like you're breezing through school without even trying. Kelsey says she does work for her grades . . . but not as hard as most of her classmates: "My good grades come naturally, so sometimes I feel guilty that my peers study all night to do good on a test, when I do well and don't study at all."

Though Kelsey knows she is different in some ways, she points out that most of all she's a regular kid: "I like to be a normal 12-year-old girl along with my 'gifted label.' I've played basketball, softball, gymnastics, bowling, dancing, and cheerleading. I love to swim, dance, and hang out with my friends."

She goes on: "If I could change something that goes on every day, I would stop the teasing and name-calling that I see around me. Sweet kids who turn mean because they are used to everyone being mean toward them. I hate watching it, so I step in.

"It breaks my heart to see kids at school hurt because of the hate that's shown to them at one of the places where you're supposed to feel safe. I think one of the reasons kids do this stuff to other kids is that they feel insecure about themselves, which is sad too."

Are there ever times when you try to hide the fact that you are gifted?

I usually don't ask too many questions or answer the teacher's questions because I don't want the other kids to feel bad that I know so much. I try to give the other kids a turn.
Boy, 5, Florida

I try to hide it sometimes in school, because I am afraid of being wrong. I know I am smart and know I should understand what is going on, and when I don't, I simply quit to hide the fact that I don't know.
Boy, 8, Indiana

> "Sometimes I like to show off a bit—might as well."

No. I am just me. Anybody who doesn't like that isn't worth bothering with.
Girl, 8, Arizona

No way, I never try to hide my intelligence because one day I am going to college with this brain.
Girl, 9, Utah

I have never tried to hide my gifted abilities from anyone. Hey, it's not my problem others have a problem with it. Sometimes I like to show off a bit—might as well.
Boy, 10, New Hampshire

No. I mean what is the reason to act dumber than you really are?
Girl, 10, Texas

My closest friends are gifted, so I don't really need to hide from them. Around other kids in my class, though, I hide my giftedness so that I won't be made fun of. When I first meet someone, I try to act average so I'm not considered too smart.
Boy, 10, Illinois

Yes, because I have a big ego and my friends call me a nerd.
Boy, 10, Florida

There are actually many times when I try to hide that I am gifted. I don't like being different or being treated differently. I don't like being asked to do people's homework for them or being called "teacher's pet." I would rather be like the person in my favorite poem: "I'm nobody, who are you?"–Emily Dickinson.
Girl, 11, Ohio

Well, I'm not embarrassed to say that I'm in GT but it is something I don't like to expose. I play football, basketball, soccer, and I'm in track. I'm as normal as the person that is next to you.
Boy, 11, Maryland

I never want to hide the fact that I'm gifted because that's just hiding one of the things that makes me me!
Girl, 11, Virginia

Not really. I sometimes overflow with terminology when talking to another kid at school. Strangely, they seem to actually understand what I am saying. And they still remember it afterward. Weird!
Girl, 11, Ohio

Sometimes I do try to hide the fact that I'm gifted. I don't want to be a nerdy brainiac and lose more friends! Trust me, I've had experience. It's not fun.
Boy, 11, Texas

No. I don't think of it as a bad thing when kids say, "Want to trade brains?" or something like that. I take it as a compliment.
Boy, 11, Michigan

No, not really. I never try to hide it. I just go by the rule, "If they don't ask, don't tell."
Girl, 11, Washington

I do sometimes hide the fact that I'm gifted because I'm not a real good person on being different. I mean, I like to wear weird things and come up with new hairstyles, but other than that, I don't like to be different.
Girl, 11, New York

No. I don't need to because I'm just showing off my gifts, like a basketball all-star shows off his gifts on the court.
Boy, 12, Oklahoma

Yeah, sometimes I really try to fit in because it makes me feel more confident. (No, I don't have issues!)
Boy, 12, Vermont

Reflection Connection

When did you first become aware of pressures to conform or fit in (for yourself or others)? How do you think a gifted person can cope with the stress associated with these pressures? Write out your ideas on a piece of paper, or draw a picture.

Do you ever do anything just to go along with the crowd? Why or why not?

No I don't. I just fit in.
Boy, 6, Texas

No, because if some don't care for the way I am, then they are the ones missing out on a good friend.
Girl, 7, Montana

Yes, because I don't like to be seen as different.
Girl, 8, Colorado

No, I just be me—wearing my flannels and cutting my hair real short. It's what I do.
Boy, 8, Iowa

No, not really. If I do everything someone else does, then who is going to be me? But sometimes, I'll do something somebody else says just to be funny or something like that.
Girl, 8, Texas

"I am a leader, not a follower."

Yes, I do because I want to blend in.
Girl, 9, Iowa

No—I make my own choices based on what I've been taught is right/wrong. If I go along with the crowd, it's because I want to (i.e., because I think it's morally okay).
Boy, 10, Illinois

Sometimes people go along with me because I should know the right way (I'm gifted after all).
Girl, 10, New Mexico

No. I am a leader, not a follower.
Boy, 10, Illinois

Sometimes, because I don't want to be an outcast.
Boy, 10, Texas

I try to be as innovative and unusual as possible just because, well, (1) I have a highly well-enforced reputation, and (2) I like it that way.
Boy, 10, Massachusetts

Yes, because then people treat me normal.
Girl, 10, Minnesota

No, I think that being independent is better than going with others. I can't explain why, I just don't like to do the same thing as others all the time.
Boy, 11, Iowa

Doesn't everybody try to fit in?
Girl, 11, Georgia

Sometimes. I get tired of being different from everyone else.
Boy, 11, Ohio

I pride myself on living the way I want to, and not the way other people want me to.
Girl, 11, Alabama

I'm almost one hundred percent me. If I tried to follow the crowd, I'd mess up and look like a loser. People accept me for who I am, and I like the people who accept me, so I leave my personality alone.
Boy, 12, Wisconsin

Yeah. I think we all do that, gifted or not. I do basically because of peer pressure. I don't think any of us are good at ignoring that!
Girl, 12, Ohio

Yes, I do, because I'm not a very forward or outgoing person and so, I sometimes wait for everyone else instead of going ahead.
Boy, 12, Vermont

I ignore my abilities and just act like anyone else to fit in with the crowd. I know that is not the right thing to do, but I just want to fit in with everyone else.
Girl, 12, New Hampshire

What is it like when you feel smarter than some of your friends?

I don't really care that I'm smarter than most of my friends.
Boy, 6, Texas

It's really hard sometimes. One of my cousins has learning disabilities so he really struggles to get stuff that I know in a heartbeat. I know it's silly, but sometimes I wish I could open my head and scoop some of my brains into his so school wouldn't be so hard for him and he wouldn't get so down on himself.
Girl, 8, New Mexico

I sometimes get impatient when they don't understand something that I think is easy. Every now and then a boast sort of pops out of my mouth.

Boy, 9, Iowa

Sometimes I get annoyed that other kids don't know as much as I do. They ask how to spell words and don't understand some of my vocabulary.

Girl, 9, Illinois

Sometimes I feel bad that I have a learning advantage over some of my friends and question why God chose to give me the abilities that He did.

Boy, 10, Illinois

I don't like being smarter than my friends.

Girl, 10, Minnesota

Sometimes when I am helping another person by explaining a problem, they still don't get it and complain that I am too complicated. I don't understand why they don't get it, and my explaining how to get the answer makes it more complicated to them than the original problem.

Boy, 10, Indiana

It's scary. My friends are two or more years older than me and a lot of times they're below me academically. It feels weird, because while they start variables and signed numbers, I study for the SAT. I read Hugo's *Les Misérables* two years ago and they have absolutely no interest in it, or any other long book.

Girl, 11, Massachusetts

I am not smarter than my friends—I find that my friendships with people who aren't able to think like me usually end.

Boy, 11, Texas

"Every now and then a boast sort of pops out of my mouth."

I always hate it when something maybe accidentally slips out of my mouth that might seem like I am bragging about being smarter than my friends.

Girl, 11, Nebraska

You get used to it. But I hate the fact that you can't confide in them about some of your problems or tell them what you REALLY like to do in your spare time.

Boy, 12, Ohio

I guess it depends on whether I attach value with intelligence. I shouldn't. Everyone has what they were born with. The most value is how much people help people, not how smart or pretty they are. Me thinking I'm better because I'm smart is just the same as someone thinking they're better because they are pretty.

Girl, 12, Alaska

Reflection Connection

Is there a question we should have asked about friends, peers, and fitting in that didn't show up in this chapter? If so, write it out and send it to us—and send us your answer too. (Our address and email address are on page 3.)

Expectations:
Too Many?

Argh! There can be a lot of expectations heaped on a gifted kid. You've got gifts, the thinking goes, so you better not waste them. Think of all the great things you're capable of!

Does this sound familiar? Do parents, teachers, and friends expect too much from you?

Expectations don't just come from others, though. Gifted kids usually expect a lot from themselves too. With all these expectations coming from without and from within, it's natural that you might feel a little pressure.

Or a lot of pressure.

Many gifted kids cope with the pressure well. They realize that perfection is impossible and mistakes are a natural part of life. They can use mistakes as an opportunity to learn, and they're not afraid to take chances on things they might not succeed at.

Others, though, have trouble with the pressure of expectations. They may hold themselves to standards they can't live up to, try to please others at all costs, or beat themselves up when they fail. That kind of pressure can lead to loneliness or sadness. See if you recognize any of your own thoughts or feelings in the quotes in this chapter.

What do you expect from a person who has your abilities?

I would think that person would be pretty smart but not always get A+.
Girl, 6, Texas

I expect myself to do very well in my schoolwork and in my sports; I especially want to do well in my study of foreign languages—I always want to get 100 percent. I do not expect my behavior to be any different from other kids; I do not think I should have to behave better than other kids my age.
Boy, 7, California

I suppose it sounds arrogant, but I expect myself to be better and faster and smarter than everybody else. I expect myself to answer the questions nobody else knows the answers to.
Girl, 8, Colorado

I expect to get good grades. I try to always be nice to kids who have trouble in school. Sometimes gifted kids are bosses and think they are better because they are smart. I think gifted kids are not better, only smarter.
Girl, 9, Ohio

4.1 on a 4.0 scale; 110 percent; 11/10—just things like that.
Boy, 10, Pennsylvania

With giftedness comes certain responsibilities: a responsibility to help others; a responsibility to help improve our society and world; and, a responsibility to make a difference in the individual lives of others.
Boy, 10, Illinois

> "I think gifted kids are not better, only smarter."

I expect them to not brag about themselves, but still be confident in themselves.
Girl, 10, Texas

To be humorous, understanding, literate, creative, helpful, kind, innovative, and poetic.
Boy, 10, Massachusetts

I am very hard on myself. The first time I failed a pretest I about flipped over.
Girl, 11, Massachusetts

I expect excellence, but not perfection. In a way it's sometimes better to have a 99 percent or 98 percent instead of 100 percent.
Boy, 11, Washington

I expect gifted kids to be more mature (sometimes) than others and have a better understanding of more things than other kids, like deeper ways of seeing connections and a love of learning.
Girl, 12, Virginia

I expect them to have friends and not dedicate their life to school. No matter how smart they are, everybody needs to have fun. You can't succeed in life with just wits, and you can't succeed in life with just friends.
Boy, 12, Wisconsin

I don't expect anything different, gifted kids shouldn't be treated differently because we're just normal kids with a little supercharger in our brains!
Girl, 12, Ohio

I expect them just to learn about whatever they are interested in and try their best, whether it be math or poetry. Who cares if they are in college at 10?
Girl, 12, Pennsylvania

What do others—adults or friends—expect from you?

My mom expects me to behave well and get done with my work; she also expects me to not be too tough on myself. My dad just expects me to behave well and not make things go to waste.
Boy, 7, California

Others expect me to work hard, do my best, be kind and compassionate, and be responsible. They expect me to be helpful and help others with work.
Girl, 7, Alabama

Strangers expect me to be a little kid and when they realize I'm not, they don't quite know what to do with me. I notice they talk to me a little louder than they need to and seem uneasy and glad when I leave.
Girl, 8, Colorado

Be happy in whatever I choose to do.
Boy, 8, Oklahoma

Adults don't really expect anything from you. They just think you're really smart and adorable. Kids, on the other hand, expect you to do everything right. If you get something wrong they roll their eyes at you. It really hurts my feelings. Also they never want to be your friend.
Girl, 9, North Carolina

Friends expect me to know all the answers and they want to be my partner at school. My parents expect my best at all times. My teacher expects me to earn 100 percent on all my schoolwork—if I don't, I lose gifted pullout enrichment activities.
Boy, 10, Illinois

They expect me to be really smart and organized. It feels like they want me to be perfect.
Girl, 10, Texas

Others think I can get all A's. They also expect me to move faster, be better organized, and have better handwriting. Geez, better handwriting?!
Boy, 10, Nebraska

I think some adults expect me to start quoting Shakespeare! One soccer coach was making fun of a neighbor's daughter whose parents punish her by taking away her books. My mom and dad just glared at him before they mentioned that is exactly what they do with ME!! It works too. I stop. The coach never really spoke to me after that. I guess we intimidated him. ☺
Girl, 11, Ohio

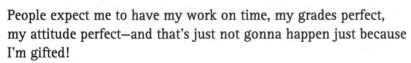

People expect me to have my work on time, my grades perfect, my attitude perfect—and that's just not gonna happen just because I'm gifted!
Girl, 11, Texas

Adults need to realize that we are just kids and gifted doesn't mean we have to have a list of expectations!
Boy, 11, Kentucky

They expect me to be perfect. For example, if my brother gets straight C's, my parents are proud of him. But unless I get straight A's, my parents don't recognize me.
Boy, 12, Oklahoma

Reflection Connection

Make a list of expectations others have for you. Can you remember if these expectations changed when you were formally identified as gifted? How do you feel about these expectations? Do you think they are reasonable? Why or why not?

How do others react when you make a mistake?
How do you react when you make a mistake?

My mom just tells me it's okay and helps me correct the mistake. My dad just cheers me up if I make a mistake (which is enough help for me). I get angry with myself and start hyperventilating and punishing myself if I make a mistake.
Boy, 7, California

Surprised, because they don't expect me to make mistakes (even though I do).
Girl, 7, Alabama

In my family everybody is pretty smart so if I make a mistake I get teased. Making mistakes makes me angry. I don't usually talk to anybody when I get that way and everybody kind of backs off until I get over it. They never really make me feel bad about it—but I sure do!
Girl, 8, Colorado

Others are disappointed in me when I make a mistake, but more when I don't try.
Boy, 8, Nebraska

"They don't expect me to make mistakes (even though I do)."

Sometimes my friends laugh or make fun of me and I feel like I'm a dummy.
Boy, 9, Illinois

I react just like anyone else—no big deal. How else will I learn if I don't make mistakes?
Girl, 9, Illinois

For most mistakes some people just point it out and I feel a slight wave of disappointment. For very big mistakes, I might burst into tears (I am an emotional person).
Girl, 10, Pennsylvania

My friends think it is okay, but other kids act like it is the end of the world.
Boy, 10, Florida

People think I shouldn't make mistakes because I'm gifted. What a crock!
Boy, 10, Idaho

Well, others are surprised—and so am I.
Boy, 10, New Mexico

When my mom sees that I got a bad grade, she gives me a lecture.
Girl, 10, Iowa

I can get pretty hard on myself when I make a mistake. It really bothers me. Mom says I have perfectionistic tendencies. I think she is right. Sometimes I get called stupid and dumb, but they call me that when I'm right so what difference does it make!
Girl, 11, Delaware

Others make wise-cracks about me and I slump down and pretend I am not there.
Boy, 11, Wisconsin

39

I usually believe that the teacher made a mistake, which is usually the case. If it was a true mistake on my part, I tell myself that I could have gotten it right if I had worked harder or had more time to study.

Girl, 11, Ohio

> "People stare at me like they are about to call the evil, killer dogs on me."

When I make a mistake other people stare at me like they are about to call the evil, killer dogs on me. I just make sure I correct it and move on . . . quickly!

Boy, 11, Iowa

I just get a little "queasy," but it doesn't happen much.

Girl, 12, Wisconsin

I feel fine when I make a mistake. But, I'm at a "gifted and talented" school, so some teachers act like the earth will explode if you make a mistake. Others treat you normal and say it happens to everyone. I like that.

Boy, 12, Ohio

When I make a mistake I feel embarrassed, probably because before I got to middle school, I got almost everything right. But I know that everyone is human (well, most everyone) and I try to remind myself to check my work, or tell myself that it's not a big deal.

Girl, 12, Wisconsin

Reflection Connection

What's the difference between trying to be perfect and trying to be excellent? How do you find yourself trying to achieve one or the other?

What do teachers expect from gifted students? Do they treat gifted students different from others? If so, how?

Teachers expect us to be at the top of the class all the time. Even when we (the GT kids) are all together in the class. Pretty tough to manage this when there is a curved grading scale and no more than 8 percent of kids can get an A in our pullout class!
Boy, 9, Ohio

My gifted teachers understand what we're going through and that we're not perfect. If we make a mistake, it's no big deal. And, we get to choose some of the projects we do. They expect us to be responsible for our learning and make conscious decisions.
Boy, 12, Ohio

> "Teachers always expect me to absolutely LOVE doing work in school."

My gifted teacher seems to be like us—gifted too. She relates to the difficulties we face when not in our pullout class. She goes to bat for us with regular teachers who expect us to make up work we miss to come to pullout. She helps us think about issues and talk freely about our concerns, and she respects differing opinions.
Girl, 12, Ohio

Teachers expect us to intuitively know how to figure things out on our own. I wish our teachers would spend a little more time explaining and less time belittling us in front of other students for not understanding and figuring things out on our own.
Boy, 12, New York

Teachers always expect me to absolutely LOVE doing work in school. Hey, I have a life too; and, I don't think they go home and do nothing except ruminate over their subject to their family all night!
Boy, 12, North Carolina

Are you pressured by parents, teachers, or others because you are gifted?

Sometimes I wish I was like other kids who don't have to work hard at school and their parents are still happy.

Boy, 7, New Mexico

My mom wants me to make money.

Boy, 8, Nebraska

Sometimes my parents or teacher expect far more from me than I can give all at once. I just want to be like everybody else. I don't want to do special lessons because I'm smarter than some people. I just want to fit in.

Girl, 8, Ohio

My teachers are always pressuring me. Just because I am gifted doesn't mean I can't make mistakes Sometimes I get really frustrated that they can't understand my feelings. I wish they could just listen to what I have to say.

Boy, 9, Alabama

No. I am accepted for who I am and not pressured. My parents are right there to help if someone begins pressuring me, like friends and especially teachers.

Girl, 9, Pennsylvania

I feel especially pressured by my peers because I am always asked to let them copy my work. My parents are also always cracking the whip if I let off a little. They say that I am gifted and that I must always be pushing myself so that my education will be more than just the standard minimum.

Girl, 10, Michigan

My parents never stop, and I hardly ever catch a break! Plus if I get one bad grade, like a B, I never hear the end of it!
Boy, 11, Georgia

I'm not pressured by people. I just think they are trying to encourage me about staying gifted. They're just trying to say they are proud of me being gifted.
Boy, 11, Ohio

My mom and dad expect me to read and do my homework in, like, 15 minutes, when we are supposed to have one hour to one and a half hours of homework. It can be very frustrating.
Girl, 11, New Hampshire

Sometimes parents or teachers think we are like Superman and we can multitask to the extreme. But we are like Spiderman: we don't know everything, and I get a little pressured and frustrated.
Girl, 11, North Carolina

My parents say I should be using my abilities at my highest level, but I think they want me to be perfect.
Boy, 12, California

Teachers and my parents think if I get a bad grade it was because I wasn't trying hard enough, or I wasn't paying attention. It gets very annoying. It is one thing having it at school, but coming home to it is a different story!
Girl, 12, Oregon

"If I get one bad grade, like a B, I never hear the end of it!"

Reflection Connection

Sometimes the pressure of expectations is so powerful it can be felt by people around you. Billy, age nine, told us this story:

I was doing well in my chess club. I moved up to a higher bracket to compete in, and was smoking my way through the competition. There was one boy, though, I knew was having some problems. His dad pushed hard each time he competed. It was all about winning.

We had made it through the preliminary rounds and were facing one another. Within our first few opening moves, I saw a way to win. Apparently, this boy saw it too. His eyes began to water and he slumped his shoulders. Add to this his dad's cheering at each move he made no matter how useless it was. I knew I would win, but to what end?

I flubbed a move and let him win. The pressure on him was too much for me to bear. I lost, but I really won. The feeling I had inside was much more important to me than moving on to the next level in the competition. I felt like a hero and knew I did something good for someone in need.

Have you ever been in a situation similar to Billy's? If so, what did you do? If not, imagine that you were Billy. What would you have done? Why?

Has anyone ever told you, "You're so smart you can do (or be) anything you want"? How does this make you feel?

Happy, because they have just told me a compliment. It definitely makes me feel happy.
Girl, 9, Pennsylvania

My friends and family ask me to do things that involve using my head. I feel like they think I am a brainiac.
Girl, 10, Florida

Yes, I have been told that I am so smart I can do anything! That gives me the power to go forth in schoolwork, to pursue and live up to my expectations. To do, and be, what I want to be when I get older. But, I'm having a hard time figuring out just what this could be.
Boy, 10, Ohio

Yes, people have said that to me before and it makes me feel kind of "too smart." I feel guilty.
Girl, 12, Ohio

Do you ever feel lonely or depressed due to your giftedness?

No, because I have a lot of friends so I don't feel lonely. Yet, every once in a while I feel depressed with the weight of the world on my shoulders.
Girl, 9, Pennsylvania

No. I never find myself lonely or depressed due to giftedness. I do find myself alone, though, but I need this time for myself.
Boy, 10, Nebraska

Of course not. Why would you? You are smarter than the average person. The only reason I could be sad is if I had no one to talk to.
Boy, 11, Illinois

I have lots of friends who are also gifted, so I don't go through life wondering about weird things without the support of other weirdos!
Girl, 12, Wisconsin

Only when someone makes fun of me, after school I go home and lock my bedroom door.
Girl, 12, Indiana

At times I do feel alone because I only have a very few friends who understand me as gifted. But, I do have a lot of friends who are very good to me (but who are not gifted).
Boy, 12, Nebraska

Yes. I feel lonely because I don't know what to talk to people my own age about. So, I never make any friends and I feel very lonely.
Girl, 12, New York

If You Are Depressed

Lots of gifted kids feel sad and lonely sometimes, but if you feel sad, lonely, or angry, and those feelings stick around for a long time, you might be depressed. If that happens to you, talk to a trusted adult right away. Talking about your feelings can help you feel better. If you can't talk to an adult in person, look in the Yellow Pages under Crisis Prevention or in the White Pages under First Call for Help. You also can call the toll-free National Youth Crisis Hotline: 1-800-448-4663. To read more about depression and sad and lonely feelings, check out *What to Do When You're Sad & Lonely* by James J. Crist, Ph.D. (Free Spirit Publishing, 2005).

A Kid Like You: Mario, Age 9

In many ways, Mario is an ordinary kid: he likes hanging out with friends and family and playing sports and games. But unlike most kids, Mario is highly gifted. His interests are different from others his age. Even when he was very young he loved math, complicated games, and anything complex. "When I was 2 years old I would lie in bed, pretend to be asleep, and count up to 300 just about every night," he says. "When I was 4, I started homeschooling and began first grade math."

Back then Mario didn't know he was different from other kids, so when he started preschool he got a surprise. "I expected other kids my age to be just like me," he says. "Wow, was I wrong."

"Mario had always been an intense baby," his mom says. "But something definitely changed between the ages of 3 and 4. He went from being a generally happy child to severely depressed. I knew something wasn't working in Mario's life but I just didn't know what exactly it was."

Mario couldn't connect with other kids his age.

"All I really remember is that when I turned 4 I stopped having friends," Mario says. "I didn't know why I didn't have friends and became very sad and lonely. I came to blame myself, believing I was stupid. Stupid people don't have any friends; therefore, it was my fault that I was lonely.

"At home my mom and brother played regular games with me like baseball and soccer. I loved to get really involved and be moving a lot. I knew all the rules, which helped me get into playing really well. When I went to preschool things were different. My friends from preschool didn't understand the games I wanted to play so we basically stopped playing. I like to know rules before we play so everyone can be fair. Most other kids just wanted to run around and play. They didn't care about doing games the right way. I didn't like to play that way, so I sat off to the side and watched."

Besides his social problems at school, Mario was unsatisfied with the classroom activities too. "All we did was glue precut pieces of paper onto other sheets of paper."

Mario had expectations for school that weren't being met, which led to a lot of frustration and anger. It also led to a new label: "I'm a preschool dropout!" Mario says.

Mario's story is pretty typical for a gifted kid his age, just beginning to realize he is different from other kids. This sense of "differentness" can lead to loneliness or even depression. It takes support from parents or other adults to help you understand your giftedness and to help you make connections with others who understand and accept you for who you are.

Mario's mom had him tested to find out why he was so sad. One of the tests showed that Mario had a high IQ, which helped him and his mom understand what was going on.

"I didn't know other kids were so different from me," Mario says. "I had to learn (and still do) how other people saw what I was doing. It's hard when I have to hold back from being me so I don't stand out like a sore thumb from other kids. I had to really slow myself down, which was hard."

> "I didn't know other kids were so different from me."

One day, while chatting on the Internet with parents of other gifted children, Mario's mom discovered one family lived near their home. They set up a meeting, and Mario made a new friend he could connect with. "Both boys wanted to play soccer," his mom says. "They sat down and talked through all the rules for 15 minutes before kicking the ball once. It was an enjoyable game for both."

Since that time, Mario has made several other friends who accept him with his differences. He met most of these through the Davidson Institute for Talent Development—a program that supports highly gifted kids and helps them meet and get to know one another. Now, Mario says, "I feel good about myself, knowing that I may not be like all kids but I'm still a good person. I know other kids who have gone through the same angry experiences I did. We really click when we get together. That makes me feel good about being me. I may not ever have lots of friends, but with the ones I do have I can be happy."

Do you feel awkward when you feel smarter than a sibling, a teacher, or even a parent?

The stuff I have to do in school I've somehow known since before I got there. It makes me sit doing nothing or coloring when I have so many questions in need of answers.

Boy, 5, Indiana

Sometimes I do feel awkward that I am smarter. It doesn't make me think they are stupid. I just think they don't know the stuff I know yet. I think they can be the same as me as long as they try.

Girl, 7, Connecticut

"Sometimes I'll ask my mom a question and she'll be totally stumped."

My parents are also very smart, so I do not feel weird.

Girl, 8, North Carolina

Sometimes I do feel awkward because I feel like a nerd around them and I do not like that feeling.

Girl, 8, Nebraska

I sure do. Teachers sometimes talk quicker and give much less detail when I ask a question. It's like they are withholding information to show their authority over me. You should remember, try not to TEACH gifted people, just let them LEARN.

Boy, 9, Georgia

Yes, because sometimes I'll ask my mom a question and she'll be totally stumped. Even when I ask my brother he looks blank; but, he's a teenager and he usually has that look.
Girl, 9, Indiana

No, I love it. I get away with anything.
Boy, 10, Japan

I don't feel awkward. When I'm in school, I'm all business—learning on my own. When I'm out of school, I'm all goofy and fun loving (not showing very much, if any, smartness).
Boy, 11, Indiana

No, I don't feel awkward because I am smarter. No one should feel weird about being smart.
Girl, 11, Oklahoma

I feel very awkward that I'm smarter than my older sister because instead of being able to ask her for help, she is asking me for help. I remember when I was in kindergarten and my older sister asked my mom if she knew how to spell *spider* and *violet*. My mom had to get out paper and I remember just spelling it out very easily. My sister said I was trying to make her feel stupid, so I tried to hide my giftedness for weeks.
Girl, 12, California

No way!!! I'm totally comfortable with being gifted. My friends/peers don't make fun of me. To them, I'm just an average 12-year-old kid. If you met me, I bet you couldn't guess I was in gifted class.
Boy, 12, Ohio

School:

Sometimes It's Great.
Sometimes It's . . .

What's school like for you? Here's what one gifted girl told us: "We need more, More, MORE! We need different things to do. Things that are challenging and interesting."

Do you find yourself asking for "more, more, more"? If you're like many gifted kids, you probably do. Gifted learners do need more—and *different*—learning opportunities than other kids their age. They may need to explore in more depth, in more breadth, and at a faster pace. Unfortunately, some schools don't offer any real opportunities for *more*. For gifted kids at these schools, life can be very frustrating. That's one reason why many gifted kids are homeschooling.

In a lot of schools the need for more *can* be met, at least to an extent. These schools may offer pullout programs, acceleration in a content area, grade skipping, resource rooms, cluster grouping, multi-age classrooms, competitions and clubs, independent study, high school and college options, or enrichment. Often, one or more of these options is enough to keep gifted kids learning and satisfied. Other times, they may help but not enough. For example, maybe teachers provide *some* challenging curriculum, but kids need *more* of it. Or gifted kids meet in pullout classes or enrichment, but they need *more* opportunities to get together (especially more than only one day a week).

And when you don't get *more*? For many, that leads to *boring*.

Gifted kids use the word *boring* a lot. If you're bored at school you're not alone—as you'll see in this chapter—but unfortunately you're also not learning. The first step to changing that is figuring out why you're bored. Is school too easy? Too hard? Is it plain uninteresting? Too repetitive? Do you get too much busywork? Do the subjects seem unconnected to your life?

Once you know why you're bored, do something about it. You are the only person who can decide if and when you learn. There are lots of ways you can take charge of your education, both in and out of school. Many gifted kids ask their teachers for more challenging spelling words, math problems, or reading assignments. With help from an adult, many find a mentor in a subject they're interested in. Others do internships. You might start a class (or school) newsletter and write news stories, complete with research and interviews, for every issue, or launch a book club or school science or math club.

In this chapter you'll read about the positive and negative learning experiences of many gifted kids. Some will probably sound familiar. Some might give you ideas!

Describe a typical and a perfect school day.

A normal school day is very easy, but a perfect school day would be challenging.
Boy, 7, Texas

A typical day would be going to school and doing some boring work. A perfect day would be on a Monday. On Monday I go to enrichment, which is my favorite place. I look forward to Mondays because I get to do challenging activities and my teacher stretches my brain.
Girl, 9, Ohio

A perfect school day would be when we don't have to do very much work except for math and writing. I would like doing nothing but math all day long.
Girl, 10, Texas

A typical day at school for me is boring because I know a lot of things we do and then I start to play when I am finished with my work. I get into trouble for playing, but I can't help it because I am bored. I would like to do science more often. We could touch and explore things more often. I would be able to get out of my seat and talk to people while I learn.
Boy, 10, Ohio

I would say that a perfect school day would be to go to school, learn something new in math, and then go to the GT program for the rest of the day.
Boy, 11, Texas

My typical school day has boring classes and super fun classes. Some of the boring classes are reading (stories too easy) and social studies (can't ask questions related to life, only the textbook). My perfect school day, I would learn new things in every class and always be challenged with different work. I would have band, choir, and chamber choir. I would be given my level of work so I would never feel like I was bored.
Girl, 12, Idaho

A perfect school day is when what the teachers are teaching is taught in a hands-on way, not just sitting there and the teacher is talking.
Girl, 12, New Jersey

A typical day in school is basically a rat race. It goes from one class to another, work, work, work. Teachers just drone on and on about nothing but junk.
Boy, 12, Maryland

What makes a perfect school day? Write out a list of your ideas, including social and academic things. Then brainstorm things you can do to make your *typical* school day more like your perfect one.

What is the biggest challenge for gifted students in school?

The hardest thing for me is handwriting. I don't even understand why it's important. It's not really learning since I can use the computer to type. It's my mind that's important to develop.
Girl, 7, Texas

We get double the homework because we are smart and expected to do more.
Girl, 10, Virginia

I think the biggest challenge for smart students is when you make a mistake and do something wrong and everyone looks at you like you're crazy and/or stupid for doing that because they expect more out of you.
Boy, 10, Texas

I think the hardest thing about being gifted in school is being made fun of because you are some nerdy brainiac!
Girl, 11, Alabama

School itself. It isn't flexible enough to allow us to grow as individuals. Everything is very structured, and if you ask for any differences you are seen as bucking the system, looking for trouble.
Boy, 11, Ohio

Excessive amounts of redundant homework.
Boy, 11, Iowa

I think the biggest challenge for smart students comes when they fail. It makes their parents or teachers disappointed and can cause them to become depressed or angry with themselves. Whenever I get a not-so-good grade, I am mad for weeks.
Boy, 12, Vermont

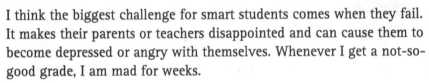

A Kid Like You: Emily, Age 7

Emily lives in Michigan, where she likes to play outside with her friends and play the piano and violin. "And annoy my little sister," she adds.

Emily has worked hard to make sure she gets the education that is right for her. When she started kindergarten, she knew right away it wasn't a good fit. "Kindergarten was too easy," she says. "I had already learned my alphabet and I could read so I didn't need to learn it again."

"Emily was convinced a mistake had been made and she had been placed in preschool," says her mom. "After six weeks, she refused to go to school."

Emily knew a change needed to be made, and she made it happen. "I talked to my mom and dad and teachers about it, and they sent me to second grade full time. I already was in

→

the second grade reading group, so I knew some of the kids and made a lot of friends."

You might think Emily was brave talking to her teachers—and she was—but she was scared too. "When the teachers talked to me I was scared, but I told them I really wanted to go to second grade."

Emily's mom was the one who called the teacher, but it was Emily who really made the grade skip happen. "I think what got the teacher's support was Emily's insistence that the grade skip was her idea, that she was ready to leave school rather than sit and never learn anything," her mom says.

> "I told them I really wanted to go to second grade."

The next school year, Emily went to a different school. "I thought it was going to be awesome because I was going into third grade. But the teacher said I had to stay in second grade." Again, Emily took charge. "I requested a meeting with my teacher to show her all of the work I had done the past year. As I got older, talking to teachers wasn't so scary."

Emily convinced the teacher to move her into third grade, but halfway through the school year she changed schools again because the work was still too easy. At her new school, though, she found herself in second grade again. "But this time some of the work was hard," Emily says. She also made friends. "Finally I found kids who liked school. No one cared that I was younger."

Soon, things changed again. "My dad got transferred to Michigan. I was excited to go to a new school, but my mom found out that I'd have to go to second grade again because I was only 7. I really didn't want to go to second grade again! This would be my third time and it was easy the first two times."

Emily did not have to attend second grade for a third time. The principal from Emily's last school (with urging from Emily's mother) contacted the new school and Emily went to third grade. Finally!

"When I was in preschool," Emily says, "I dreamed about going to second grade. I didn't know that I'd be there for so long."

What happens to you in school that makes learning more difficult or less interesting?

When we have to do essays that follow a specified pattern. This is so boring!
Girl, 9, Illinois

Projects! Not all of them, just the busywork ones where I have a lot of cutting and pasting to do to make something look neat, but I don't exercise my brain muscle to learn anything.
Boy, 11, Arizona

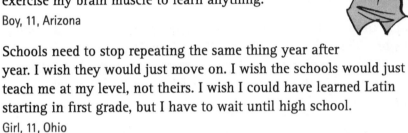

Schools need to stop repeating the same thing year after year. I wish they would just move on. I wish the schools would just teach me at my level, not theirs. I wish I could have learned Latin starting in first grade, but I have to wait until high school.
Girl, 11, Ohio

In social studies you sit and sit and do more sitting and it's really dull because all you're doing is looking at books. You don't do much standing up or moving around (unless you bring up a contradiction to the book from life—then you get to go to the office).
Girl, 12, Wisconsin

One year we were in a math class that was way ahead of everybody else. The next year in math we all practically knew everything and the teacher didn't do one thing about it.
Boy, 12, Iowa

We need more interaction with one another to fully remember and understand what we are learning. If I am taking a test and am stumped on a question, it's easier to think back to activities and remember than it is to think back to when we were taking notes and I was about to fall asleep.
Girl, 12, Ohio

When I get bored, my brain short circuits and I enter dreamland and imagination. This, of course, does little to help me when it comes to test time, however.
Boy, 12, Maine

What activities or methods do teachers use that make learning worthwhile?

Sometimes a "hands-on" activity sure makes the day more interesting.
Boy, 7, Indiana

Well, not to be mean or anything, but my teachers don't make learning worthwhile. I'm so bored in classes all the time (except science and history). I think that the teachers should try to put some fun things in the classroom and I think that it would stick in our heads better.
Girl, 9, Oklahoma

My second period teacher is always cooking up new labs for science, and my third period teacher is reading us novels, one per month.
Girl, 10, Texas

They don't really use anything to make school fun. Duh, it's junior high.
Boy, 11, Iowa

I think playing games or making jokes or relating what we're learning to something we like makes learning worthwhile. But when we do stuff straight out of the book, it is soooooo boring!!!!
Girl, 12, Ohio

Having a sense of humor doesn't hurt one bit.
Girl, 12, Ohio

I think reading on your own is good, because you get to read better and faster, and the whole time you are usually enjoying a book. (I'm not talking about textbooks.)
Boy, 12, Maine

Anything other than lecture, lecture, lecture.
Boy, 12, Ohio

Do you ever get bored in school? If no, why not? If yes, what do you do to relieve the boredom?

When I get bored, I try to write my name or my friend's name backwards or I read or draw.
Boy, 5, Florida

I don't really do anything but think to myself because that's all I can do. My teacher doesn't like it when we daydream.
Girl, 7, Texas

I draw pictures of horses, my teacher, or hockey (my future career).
Girl, 9, Michigan

I sit there and partially listen so I can raise my hand once in a while. My mind is busy daydreaming during that time.
Boy, 9, Iowa

I try to sneak open a book and do some reading.
Girl, 10, Pennsylvania

To relieve my boredom, I just look up to where the teacher is teaching and make it look like I am interested but really be thinking about something else. Or, if I can get ahead of the teacher without anyone noticing I do.
Boy, 10, Texas

I don't get bored, because the things I learn are interesting and I know that I need to listen because I may need to know those things later on in life.
Girl, 10, Louisiana

I talk and play around, like take things out of my desk (erasers, pencils, little pieces of paper) to play with. I've made a little town almost to scale out of notebook paper and eraser crumbs.
Boy, 10, Alberta, Canada

I never get bored at school. You never can. You always have something to do, and if not, read a book. That is never boring.
Girl, 10, Iowa

Usually when a teacher is lecturing on lessons and stuff, I like to take out my journal and start doodling. I still listen to the teacher, of course, but at the same time I am goofing off.
Boy, 11, California

I try to read but this makes my teachers angry!
Boy, 11, Maryland

If I get bored in school I'll either stare at one thing until the bell rings or I, uh . . . pass notes. Every kid does. There isn't any innocent little child who doesn't pass notes when bored.
Girl, 12, Ohio

To relieve the boredom I doodle on my paper and try to look like I'm so very amazed by old information.
Boy, 12, Virginia

Reflection Connection

What is the most common reason the kids you read about in this chapter are bored in school? What would you recommend they do to relieve the boredom? If school is boring for you too, why do you think that is? What can you do to relieve your boredom?

A Kid Like You: Louis, Age 9

Louis lives in New Jersey with his mom, dad, younger brother Ross, and their cat Logan. He loves the theater, especially musicals. "I have been performing in plays since I was 6," he says. "It is great fun to get up on a stage and sing, dance, and perform." He also likes to ride his bike and play tennis with his dad. "And I spend as much time on the computer as my parents will let me," he adds.

When Louis started school he struggled, for reasons he and his family didn't understand at first. But it didn't take long to figure out what was wrong.

"I entered kindergarten reading with confidence," he says. "I did not have the chance to learn much at school. I learn much faster than others and I understand material that is at a higher level than children my age or even some adults."

His parents were surprised to learn he was gifted. "Since Louis was our first child, we were not aware that he was so different," his mom says.

Louis's teachers didn't do much to help him. Instead of finding more challenging work for him, they asked him to help teach other students. "One teacher asked me to read to the class in first grade while she prepared the next lesson," Louis says. "She even told the kids to ask me if they needed help with assignments! She thought giving me a job would make me feel better about not learning. I didn't mind helping the teacher, but I wanted to learn too."

> "It would be better if schools would work to serve gifted kids' unusual needs."

It was hard for Louis to sit through hours of class without learning anything new or interesting, and his boredom eventually led to behavior problems. This got the attention of teachers, of course, but it didn't make school better for Louis.

→

Louis eventually switched schools and skipped ahead two years, and he was accelerated another two years in math. He feels challenged now and is much happier. "Until last year, I could only learn math at home," he says. "Schools would not allow me to study at the level that I am capable. It would be better if schools would work to serve gifted kids' unusual needs."

If you are frustrated with school like Louis was, he has some advice: "Don't give up when your school isn't doing all they should. You deserve the chance to learn something new at school every day!"

What could teachers do to make school a better place to learn for smart students like you?

They could allow each kid to follow interests and go at their own pace.
Boy, 7, Connecticut

Have fun projects and big schoolwide activities.
Boy, 9, Iowa

Poll students to see what they already know and then not repeat that stuff over and over.
Boy, 9, Illinois

If we get really good grades, we should get time to do puzzles or something of our choice. And, I'd like to move on if I get 100 percent on something and others don't. We should go on more field trips (even just outside) to learn about how things work instead of just the textbook.
Boy, 10, Ohio

Just treat each student the way they need to be treated. We are not all the same, but that is how the teachers treat us—like equals—but we are not! I just wish to be treated like me.
Girl, 11, Ohio

Teachers could give us more art-related projects. After all, art does help your learning ability. Also, getting to know the students personally does make kids more confident.
Boy, 11, Ohio

Teach us how to study. I can memorize, but that's about it. I worry that I'll need to know how to do something else when I come up against a subject I've never seen before. What will I do?
Girl, 11, Texas

Teachers could make school better by not giving homework, because if I can get a good grade on the test what's the point? The kids have to do the homework and the teachers have to check it. So it would be even faster if we didn't have homework, except for essays and stuff like that that teaches you how to write coherently.
Boy, 11, Iowa

Encourage everyone to work at the speed that works for them. This way, when I speed along, the other students aren't stressed by being competitive and then won't make fun of me to keep me with the pack.
Girl, 12, Minnesota

They should not expect so much out of us. The way I see it, we are just like any other kid except we have more opportunities and deep thoughts than other kids do. Sometimes I like these thoughts to get a chance to wander instead of having to deal with more piled on work.
Girl, 12, Pennsylvania

"Teachers could give us more art-related projects. After all, art does help your learning ability."

Teachers could give more options to gifted children. For example, my English teacher told my parents I was welcome to write about whatever I wanted whenever she had given the class a specific topic. Gifted kids don't need as many limitations as children that aren't.
Boy, 12, Maine

Reflection Connection

Many gifted people are complex thinkers. This can be a problem in school when you're expected to memorize simple facts. You might have experienced something like this on a test, where you studied and knew the answers but in the heat of the moment your mind went blank. Or you looked at the possible answers and could see how every one could be correct!

Cleo, a gifted girl we know, read the following question on a test:

Based on your experience and our reading, which one of the following is the main reason for the Civil War in the United States?

    a. Slavery
    b. Class differences between the North and South
    c. Economic inequality
    d. The change from agriculture to industry

Says Cleo: "Here's how I thought about which answer was best to make:

Okay, I remember the book saying that slavery was the main reason, but during yesterday's review our teacher did talk about Southerners feeling that the North was trying to destroy the way of life of the South. To me this means b. is also correct.

And, when I watched PBS last night, the show on the Civil War said the change in life from agrarian to industrial ways of life was a major cause for the conflict leading to the Civil War. And, in our GT class, we've all been talking about how the economy can only continue to grow if people are convinced they should continue

⟶

to buy things made here in this country. Since the South was pretty self-sufficient with their plantations, but cotton crop prices were falling, maybe it really WAS economic inequality that caused the Civil War.

All the answers are right. But which one is the best answer?

I ended up choosing b because it seemed to be the most general idea that all the other answers could fall under as categories. I got the question wrong. The answer was a.

I explained my answer to the teacher, but she said my thinking was way off base and everyone knew slavery was the main reason. I never argued about an answer I got wrong on a test again that year. I felt so dumb for not knowing the obvious."

Have you ever had an experience similar to Cleo's? Has this experience changed the way you do things in your life? What advice would you give Cleo?

Some schools have special programs and teachers for gifted students. Is this a good idea? Why?

I think it is a good idea, but one major problem is my school doesn't have a program until fourth grade, and kids need stuff way before that!
Boy, 6, Ohio

I think it's a good idea especially if the teachers were gifted kids themselves. They (the teachers) could give some useful tips to their students about getting along with other kids.
Boy, 7, California

I think it's a good idea so gifted kids can learn new things rather than repeating the things they already know. It helps me get to know other gifted kids and keeps me from disrupting the other kids in class.
Girl, 8, Virginia

I think yes because it gives gifted kids the opportunity to be around kids who have abilities closer to their own. It doesn't matter if they are younger or older or the same age, but they get to hang out and do more challenging projects and it's a lot of fun.
Girl, 9, Florida

I think it is good to have some special classes, but not all of them. Math and science are the only courses that should be GT because they are the two courses you need most in life. I have had to have GT classes on every subject and it is too hard and complicated with everyone breathing down your neck.
Boy, 10, Oklahoma

I think a special program is a good idea because it allows you to be creative without being picked on for being a nerd or coming up with a different way of doing or seeing something that drops regular classmates' mouths to the floor, causing them to call me names!
Boy, 10, Tennessee

I really like my gifted teacher. He seems to be the only teacher I have that really understands all of us and treats us as individuals. I know some of us have a goofy sense of humor, but with him we are safe. It is okay to be ourselves. No other teacher seems to accept us this much.
Girl, 11, Ohio

Kids who are more intelligent than others shouldn't be stuck in a class teaching other kids stuff they have already grasped. They need to learn new and more challenging things.
Boy, 11, Kansas

A gifted program is good because it increases the dendrites in your brain.
Girl, 11, Texas

Yes, I mean it is nice to be with your friends but sometimes you just need to be with people like yourself. It is really nice to be able to sit down and have an intelligent conversation.
Girl, 12, Illinois

I would rather be able to do stuff like all the other kids and not have to make up the work I miss the day I go to my program.
Girl, 12, Ohio

It's better to have SOMETHING. But it singles those kids out as nerds. It would be better to just have everyone work at their own pace, all the time, without anyone making a big deal out of it.
Girl, 12, Michigan

I moved away from a city with a self-contained gifted program. Now I realize how lucky I was because now I learn almost nothing.
Boy, 12, Ohio

Reflection Connection

What advice would you give a student who is considering joining your gifted program at school? After you answer, ask a gifted friend to answer also. Compare your results and discuss what it would be like for a new person coming into your school's gifted program. What could you do as a team to help make it easier for the new person?

If you're in a gifted program, how do you feel about it?

I like it because we get to learn about different stuff than other kids.
Boy, 6, Texas

WOO HOO. It's a thrill a minute!
Boy, 7, Indiana

I go to a school that individualizes curriculum (a private school after leaving a public school). I love my school because the kids are nice, the work is fun, I am expected to work hard and produce my best work, I am challenged to learn, and learn to love learning.
Girl, 7, Michigan

I wish I was there more than just one day a week. The teachers and activities are wonderful, and I get to know more about me in a place where it is all right to be me.
Boy, 8, North Carolina

This program helps me use the extra knowledge that I have. If there was no gifted program at my school, I don't know what I would do to help me. A program like this should be in every school around the globe.
Boy, 10, Ohio

I'm recognized as gifted at my school, but we no longer have a gifted program, and I miss the challenging activities that we used to do. School is not as interesting without the program.
Boy, 10, Illinois

"I wish I was there more than just one day a week."

The program needs to be more than one day a week. I'm gifted the other days too!
Boy, 10, Wisconsin

I love the program. We get to really research a subject area that only gets touched on (or repeated a thousand times) in our regular class. We get to be together with a teacher who just understands us and lets us be ourselves. He encourages us to take chances and not be afraid of things not working out.

Girl, 11, Ohio

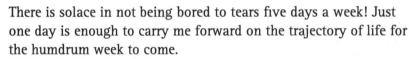

I think it is great, but it needs to be expanded. Why not Latin? History and language arts all in one?

Boy, 11, Wisconsin

There is solace in not being bored to tears five days a week! Just one day is enough to carry me forward on the trajectory of life for the humdrum week to come.

Boy, 11, Indiana

I feel great encouragement from other gifted students and I feel that it has opened me to a whole new world of thinking. It gives me a chance to show my ability by expressing my ideas to people who understand where I am coming from.

Girl, 12, Ohio

Sometimes I have a lot of makeup work. It really tires me out to be penalized for being accepted into the program and then having to make up work I miss in my regular class.

Boy, 12, Minnesota

The program we have isn't enough. I go there, and it's okay, and it's nice to get out of the horrible monotony of class. But it isn't much better. I still ace most of the stuff. A lot of it is just boring memorization, which isn't harder than in normal class, just more.

Girl, 12, Nebraska

I LOVE THE PROGRAM!!!! You get to go at a faster pace. I just wish we had the program every day instead of only once a week.
Girl, 12, Ohio

What do you do in gifted programs? Do these things make sense? Explain.

"Right now we're casting for a movie we're making."

We spend a lot of time working on projects, painting murals, and listening to music. I don't learn anything and wish I could choose what to do. Instead, we get assigned projects and don't do really anything interesting to me.
Girl, 9, Indiana

We only get to do GT work once a week. This makes absolutely no sense to me. I'm gifted EVERY day, not just once a week. And, I get punitive fallout for attending our pullout program because I have to make up the work I missed in the regular class anyway. This makes no sense to me.
Boy, 11, Ohio

Right now we're casting for a movie we're making. This makes sense, because I get to see how Hollywood works and I'd never get that chance in regular classes.
Girl, 12, Utah

A few of the projects we do are pointless, like rewriting the constitution for a grade. We are forced, not voluntarily, to use our intelligence so we could better understand a subject the teacher knows less about than us. Does that make sense?
Boy, 12, Pennsylvania

In GT class we do more creative thinking than other classes and do more reports. We get to choose the type of projects and how much we want to go into them. We grade each other and do a community fair where we share what we're learning about with other people (mostly

adults). All of the regular kids think we're weird for being so interested in school things. It makes sense to me because I am learning about things I pick and can move at a speed that matches my interests.
Girl, 12, Colorado

A Kid Like You: Richard, Age 12

Richard lives in a town in western Germany called Solingen, which is known for its many knife and scissors manufacturers. Solingen also has many museums and historic buildings, including a medieval castle called Schloss Burg that was built in the early 1100s on a mountain overlooking the Wupper River. Richard lives in an apartment with his parents and 10-year-old brother, Peter.

School for Richard is probably a lot like school for you and other gifted kids in North America. When he began public school he found it too easy and boring. When he learned he was gifted at the beginning of second grade, he accelerated to third grade. "Now learning wasn't any longer so boring," Richard says. "But the new classmates were all older and bigger than me. They bullied me and made jokes about my size."

Even though Richard faced bullying, he craved an education that was challenging. It turned out the one-year jump was not enough, so he and his family began to search for a high school that would meet his needs. (In Germany, high school begins in the fifth grade.)

> "It's nice to have so many gifted classmates."

"My personal selection criterion for high school was that I wouldn't have to skip again, that I would be together with equally smart classmates, and that there would be additional interesting extracurricular activities," Richard says. "Four of the five schools we explored didn't qualify: either there was no gifted program, not enough teachers being informed about giftedness, or the gifted program started only in the seventh grade. One was of the opinion that there are no gifted kids but only conceited parents."

After looking at five schools and growing more and more frustrated, Richard's mother read about a school that specialized in teaching the gifted, called the Werner-Heisenberg Gymnasium. One problem, though: it was in a town called Leverkusen—more than an hour away by train and bus. Still, Richard and his family had a look.

According to Richard, the school seemed like it would meet his needs. "Every year they have a fifth class starting with two foreign languages at the same time," he says. "Very gifted kids can start with Japanese in the sixth grade. Additionally, they have a choir, an orchestra, a chess group, a natural-science research group, and a lot more extracurricular activities. In this class approximately half of the kids are gifted and some teachers are specially trained."

Richard and his family made the decision to attend Werner-Heisenberg Gymnasium. The experience for Richard was worth the effort.

"I think this school is great because it offers so many possibilities. It's nice to have so many gifted classmates. A lot of our teachers are instructed in teaching gifted kids, and some are gifted themselves. But there are also others: they can't imagine or they don't care that we want other things than the 'normal' kids. For example, more practical experimenting or less repetition. Because in my class are also 'normal' kids, we have to do a lot of repetition, which is boring for my friends and me."

Richard's closing comments show that gifted kids everywhere face many of the same issues: "If I could change something at school, I would take care that the classes are sorted by the pupil's speed of learning. Then the one part of the pupils would have more time and the other part wouldn't be so bored. The quicker pupils could use the gained time for learning even more or going home and following their own interests."

What makes a teacher a "gifted teacher"?

Somebody who is a good listener.
Boy, 7, Connecticut

Someone who is okay with me knowing more than them.
Boy, 9, Indiana

I think gifted teachers really get to know their students. They give a child a person to talk to and confide in, almost like a counselor. A gifted teacher will go beyond learning through a textbook, actually letting the student research freely.
Boy, 10, Ohio

A great sense of humor, a high IQ (so we can connect), a love of learning, and a passion for life.
Girl, 10, Illinois

Be able to say he or she doesn't know an answer. But, be willing to learn about the question and find the answer with the students. Not just say, "What do you think?"
Boy, 10, Virginia

The ability to live with the eccentricities of gifted students.
Girl, 10, Iowa

Being in a gifted class when they were kids.
Boy, 11, Iowa

Someone who is as excited about teaching as I am about learning.
Girl, 12, Idaho

A gifted teacher is creative, crazy, fun, not stuffy, wild-eyed, and pretty loud.
Boy, 12, Indiana

73

In the classroom everyone is learning together instead of the teacher just trying to pour information into our heads.
Boy, 12, Virginia

A pun master. This teacher gets inside jokes that crack up the gifted kids but cause regular teachers and most other kids to stop and stare.
Girl, 12, Kansas

If you could fix school for gifted kids, what would you do?

I would make it so that I could look things up any time.
Girl, 7, Texas

I would get every kid a laptop computer.
Boy, 9, Iowa

I would make sure the GT kids would have their own table at lunch.
Girl, 10, Indiana

I would make school much faster instead of working on something for weeks. I would make the days shorter instead of just filling up my daydreaming tank.
Boy, 11, Iowa

Do more hands-on activities and take trips outside to relate what we are learning to life. Be more specific showing how what we are learning is important to know now, not just preparation for a class I might take in the future.
Boy, 12, Indiana

I would give more chances for band and choir and other musical stuff and have classes where you learn stuff. And if you move through a class and pass it during the middle of the school year, that would be okay.
Girl, 12, Idaho

Home:
Life with Family

You're not just gifted at school, are you? Of course not. Even though most people think of giftedness as academic ability, gifted kids are gifted all the time. This chapter is about your home life: your relationship with your family and how you spend your free time.

Do you get pressure from family to excel in everything you do? Is a B or B+ just not good enough? Does your dad or mom brag about you? Many gifted kids could answer a resounding YES—and that kind of pressure is stressful! For some kids, the pressure leads to perfectionism, that feeling that anything less than perfect is a failure. For others, it can lead to anger or depression.

Yes, family can stress you out, but family also can help you. For most kids, family is the best source of *support* for the things that make them stressed, like school and fitting in. Sometimes it might seem like you spend most of your time arguing with siblings and parents, but their unconditional love and acceptance helps you feel good about being you.

For many gifted kids, the unconditional love of pets is another source of support. So is downtime—time when you're alone and doing pretty much nothing. Sometimes, nothing's better than doing nothing!

Finally, lots of gifted kids use their free time to get involved in community service. It feels great to know you're helping beautify your community or making a difference in another person's life.

How does your family deal with your giftedness?

Mom and Dad switched me to fourth grade instead of third. They ask my teacher for special homework. They have extra meetings with my teachers and school because they want me to have special things to do in school. They buy special books and workbooks.
Girl, 8, Ohio

We visit other gifted people and go to conferences with other gifted people.
Girl, 9, Pennsylvania

They make me study every night. I'm supposed to know more than everyone else and keep proving it.
Boy, 11, Ohio

"I'm just me to them with all my quirkiness, deep thoughts, and runs of emotions."

My parents don't really have to "deal" with it. I'm just me to them with all my quirkiness, deep thoughts, and runs of emotions. Maybe they're just used to it?
Girl, 11, Montana

My family thinks I should always act serious and shouldn't goof off. Hey, I'm a kid!
Boy, 11, Wisconsin

They treat me the same. My parents are gifted too!
Boy, 11, New York

My family is very supportive. My dad will listen when I need to talk to him about Latin or life in general. My brother looks up to me. And my mom—the most wonderful person you could ever meet. She will drive me to competitions and places where I have to take tests (like the Johns Hopkins Talent Search Test or the Hannah Orleans Test). My family backs me 110 percent!
Girl, 11, New Hampshire

My family doesn't treat me any differently, but my dad is always like, "You go girl!" when I show him my report card.
Girl, 12, Ohio

Reflection Connection

Being gifted is stressful. You can see it in many of the responses in this book, even when the word "stress" isn't used. Write a recipe for other gifted kids to help them cope with stress in their lives. Here's an example:

Recipe for Less Stress

1 whole friend
1 neighborhood block or park
13 smiles each day (you have an unlimited supply you know!)

Directions:

1. If your temperature begins to rise, pause a moment and smile. Find a friend to talk to and explain what is stressing you out.

⟶

2. Smile at every person you pass or meet. And, when you can, smile at yourself in the mirror. Smile, smile, smile: this ingredient helps others feel happier and less stressful too!

3. If none of this works, run around your block or a local park two times—exercise burns off lots of stress.

4. Continue to mix and add to your ingredients as needed.

Is anyone else in your family gifted? How do you know?

My mommy, stepfather, grandparents, aunts, and uncles are all gifted! They told me when I joined Mensa that I was the third generation of Mensa in our family.
Boy, 5, Florida

Two of my four brothers are gifted and I know that because I have heard my mom and dad talking about it in the kitchen.
Boy, 9, Maine

My mom and dad are both gifted. I know because my dad said he used to be in the gifted program at school. My mom is also because she took a test to see if she could get into Mensa and she passed the test.
Girl, 12, Ohio

How much time do you spend with your family? What do you do during this time?

I have family time when I come home from school until I go to bed. I like to paint with my mommy or do science experiments with her. Sometimes I read to her or she reads to me. I play Legos with my stepdaddy and he teaches me about computers.
Boy, 5, Florida

We have some family time, mostly on weekends. We talk, play cards, and tell jokes.
Girl, 8, Georgia

Little if any family time. My parents are very busy with work. We're lucky to see each other as a whole family before it's time for bed. Overscheduled is an understatement.
Girl, 10, Massachusetts

I have zero time for my family. I am too busy with sports and extracurricular activities. If I had time I would spend it doing homework.
Boy, 11, Wisconsin

During the school year things get really busy with soccer, piano, clarinet, and school. We only have family time in the summer.
Girl, 11, Indiana

I have a lot of family time. We go bowling, take bike rides, or do other things. Never do we watch TV (but a movie every now and then is a good thing).
Boy, 12, Michigan

Reflection Connection

Getting outdoors and away from schedules and responsibilities is a great way for families to connect. Think of three outdoor activities you can do with your family in the next week. Talk about them with your family, choose one, and do it. Afterward, ask each person to answer the following questions and share their results.

1. How did doing the activity make you feel?

2. What did you like and not like about the activity?

3. What should we do next?

Do family adults brag about your abilities or compare you to your brothers or sisters? How do you feel about these compliments or comparisons?

These compliments make me feel awesome. It feels like someone just gave me a birthday present or prize. It boosts my confidence.
Boy, 8, Indiana

Yes, I do catch my parents bragging about me to family and friends. Sometimes I feel proud that they think so much of me, but other times I get tired of it and just want to be thought of as a regular person. I sometimes feel pressured to do exceptionally well in some things just to please my parents.
Girl, 9, North Dakota

I feel great. Once they say one compliment, they go on and on and on and on and on and on . . .
Boy, 10, Texas

I don't like them bragging about me because I feel bad about the people they brag to. They might be putting down the other person's daughter or son. It's like saying that their daughter or son is dumb compared to me.
Girl, 11, Illinois

> "Once they say one compliment, they go on and on and on and on and on and on . . ."

Every time he sees me, my dad tells me that I am the smartest kid in the world. He tells everyone who meets me that too. I know that I am not, but it makes me feel special.
Boy, 12, Maine

Yes, and it BUGS me! I mean I like being complimented and all, it's just that I don't like being bragged about.
Girl, 12, Florida

Sometimes my mom tells my older sister to be more like me. Sometimes I feel good about it and other times I know my sister will get mad and not talk to me for a week.
Girl, 12, Virginia

What have family adults done to get you interested in new topics, and what haven't they discussed with you that you believe they should?

My parents sometimes bring me pamphlets about certain activities that might interest me. I do feel, and am quite embarrassed to say, that I think my parents should talk to me about the birds and the bees.
Girl, 9, Texas

My parents try to get me interested in some things by offering me rewards. When offering rewards fails they give me a lecture on how important doing new things is for my future. I wish they would include creative things to do instead of just academic things.
Boy, 9, Louisiana

My parents talk to me about everything. Sometimes too much—especially algebra! We go to lots of events, read and read some more, and they include me in conversations with other people who live differently.
Girl, 11, Texas

When I was a young child, my parents would read to me every day, and they showed me how much fun it could be. I think that this has a major effect on me today.
Boy, 12, West Virginia

They should talk to me about growing up and its troubles.
Girl, 12, Michigan

My mom is always trying to get me to read new books that I don't care for.

Girl, 12, Wisconsin

My mom bought me all of these animal books that she is trying to get me to read, but they are not interesting to me.

Boy, 12, Alabama

I think my parents need to discuss with me that they're proud of me and they are proud of what I have tried to accomplish.

Girl, 12, Ohio

Pretend you are your parent or another family member. What does giftedness mean to you? What do you expect from a gifted kid? Write a letter to you (the kid) explaining those expectations.

What have adults in your family said to you about being gifted? What expectations do they have of you because of your abilities?

My parents say that being gifted is something that will get me far in life, and that I have to appreciate it. They don't think of me as a child but as an adult who just seems smaller than them. My parents expect me to do VERY well in things. They also expect me to be more responsible than average kids.

Boy, 8, Ohio

My dad once playfully teased me that I was probably the only kid in the world who would buy a language arts workbook with a gift receipt.

Girl, 8, Pennsylvania

My parents have way too many expectations—but don't all parents? What bugs me most is they expect me to do all the busywork at school, even though they agree it is usually pointless for me.

Girl, 11, Texas

They expect me to be a straight-A student. Which I should be, considering I am, but the thing is they're disappointed with a B+.

Boy, 11, North Carolina

My parents have high expectations of my abilities. They expect me to go to a really good school on a scholarship for grades and sports. And I don't mind these expectations, I push myself to live up to them.

Girl, 12, Iowa

My parents expect me to get PERFECT grades being gifted and all, but I get average grades. They say I need to do better, and I try, but my grades stay the same. I must be some disappointment.

Boy, 12, Ohio

Reflection Connection

Write a letter to a parent or another family member sharing what, if anything, about being gifted is stressful for you. Put the letter aside for a week, then read it over again. Make any changes you feel are needed. Finally, deliver the letter to the family member—if you want to!

Who or what makes you happiest at home?

My mommy makes me happy because she always helps me do science experiments. I like to do experiments every day and my teacher doesn't do them at school.

Boy, 5, Florida

My cat Toby makes me happy. He is so lovable all the time. I also like being alone and when my parents give me space.
Girl, 8, Texas

I love to build car models. I am a girl and I do find cars interesting. I also enjoy drawing, which I feel brings out my innermost thoughts. Of course, and it is a girl's must, I love talking on the phone with my friends.
Girl, 9, New Mexico

The thing that makes me the happiest is music. Whenever I go home I always listen to music. For me it creates another world that I could just escape to. It can also inspire me when I do a project for school. Some of my best projects have come from that.
Boy, 9, Washington

I would have to say that the thing that makes me happiest is the computer, which is why I'm on it right now.
Boy, 11, Texas

What makes me happy at home is a big bowl of ice cream and my Play Station 2 (just like a normal 11-year-old boy).
Boy, 11, Iowa

> "The thing that makes me the happiest is music."

What used to make me happy was my dog. He was the only one who let me read books to him. Of course my mom and dad did too, but he really listened.
Girl, 12, New Hampshire

My quality time with myself makes me happiest at home.
Boy, 12, Arizona

What makes me happiest at home is knowing that I have a place to go and people who love me for who I am.
Girl, 12, South Carolina

Kind of just when I'm up in my room alone. I can just be myself up there and nobody will ask me what I'm doing because when they do that I feel like I'm weird because it's hard to explain and I feel childish.

Girl, 12, Iowa

A Kid Like You: Jamie, Age 10

To Jamie, *family* means an unconventional mix of people. "I have what is called an open adoption," she says. "This means that I have contact with my birth mother and we are free to visit each other if we want."

Jamie was adopted when she was 5 weeks old. When she was almost 4, her adoptive parents got divorced. "It was really hard for me," Jamie says of the divorce. "I felt the divorce was my fault, but now I know it wasn't. They just couldn't live together anymore."

Now Jamie lives with her adoptive mom and stepdad. They have two cats and four flying squirrels as pets. "We're hoping to have baby flying squirrels soon," she says. Jamie sees her dad, stepmom, and two stepsisters every other weekend. "Sometimes my adoptive mom sends pictures and letters to my birth mother, but she doesn't always get an answer back," she says. "I don't know who my birth father is. I wish I did so I could learn more about myself."

Jamie went to public school from kindergarten through third grade, but she had some problems. She explains: "I was always above my grade level for reading and always below my grade level in math. I had some problems with bullies and teasing at school and on the bus. I had a hard time paying attention in class because I have ADD (attention deficit disorder) and would get far behind. When my class would go to recess or do other fun things, I couldn't join them because I had too much work to

⟶

catch up on. I didn't get to go out and run around, and I had to sit still at my desk during the day.

"It felt like I was being punished because I couldn't do what I was expected to do at the same time and in the same way everyone else was doing it."

After third grade, Jamie and her mom made the decision to homeschool. Now things are going much better. "I'm glad I homeschool," Jamie says, "because I can move around while I'm working and I get to go on field trips and do other fun things instead of being punished for not working like other kids. Now, my math is above grade level, and I am doing well with my schoolwork every day. But I still have a hard time with spelling."

Besides the academic improvement, homeschooling has brought Jamie and her mom closer together. "My mom is my teacher, and she has taught me a lot about school and life. She is always there to make me feel better when I am down. She makes me laugh, and helps me cope with things in life that are hard."

> "My mom is always there to make me feel better when I am down."

For Jamie, and for all kids who are homeschooled, the academic side of giftedness is wrapped up intimately with the family side. If your family pressures you to perform at a high level, this can be very stressful. Luckily for Jamie, her family is pretty grounded. "My mom always knew I was bright, but she never treated me any differently because of it, or actually told me I was 'gifted.'"

Instead of pressure, Jamie gets support from her family—and humor. "My stepdad owns a trucking company and he likes to tease me that someday I will own it, but that's not my dream. My goal in life is to be an actress. I love to watch movies, and especially the special features and diaries about how the movies were made."

Jamie also gains personal satisfaction in helping others. Two nights a week she and her mom volunteer at a neurofeedback program for underprivileged kids.

"I help kids who have hard family lives and need help," she explains. "We teach them calming breathing so they can control their anger, frustration, or sadness. We also do art with them, which helps them to get some frustrations out. I also do the breathing myself because it helps me get in control of my emotions."

Jamie's passion for helping others comes from knowing that not everyone has the chances she does to succeed. In her words:

"I feel very lucky to have the opportunities that I have, because some kids don't have these opportunities. I think if you believe in your dreams and follow your heart, you can accomplish anything you want. You just have to believe in yourself and never give up."

Reflection Connection

Jamie is like many gifted kids who do service projects or volunteer in their communities. Is there anything in your community that you'd like to become involved with? Maybe something makes you proud and you'd like to spread the word about it. Or maybe something is a problem that you'd like to address. Think of an issue you're interested in, then figure out how you can get involved. Next, make it happen. Following are a few examples of ways to help (get a parent's permission first). Can you think of others?

1. Write a letter to the editor of your local paper and send it in.
2. Participate in (or organize!) a local rally for a good cause.
3. Clean an elderly neighbor's yard.
4. Clean up a local park.

How are you involved in your community? Do you think more gifted kids should get involved in their communities?

I'm involved by doing service projects with Girl Scouts, helping the Cat Angel Network at our local pet store, and collecting old cell phones to donate. I also helped my sister collect baby stuff for underprivileged pregnant moms.
Girl, 9, Pennsylvania

I'd like to do more community work. I used to do this when I was little. Now, I have too many extracurricular things going on. I want to find a way to do more though.
Girl, 11, Indiana

I am pretty involved. I think this is something a lot of students should do. It gives them a chance to connect with other people, and not just be focused on as "gifted."
Girl, 12, Michigan

I think it is hard to do this with all the stuff I already do. I'm expected to focus on schoolwork and get the best grades I can.
Boy, 12, Colorado

I cleaned up our local park and got businesses around it to donate money for flowers and plants. I also got our local hardware store to help me make benches and a sign.
Boy, 12, Virginia

Passions:
What Do You Like?

Many gifted kids we know are creative, and many have a passion—an intense interest in a subject, craft, or pastime. When involved in highly engaging subjects, gifted kids tend to have an uncanny drive for exploring deeper and deeper.

Many kids who are committed to a passion are seen as underachievers at school because they don't perform at their best there. They often do just well enough to earn marks that keep teachers and parents off their backs. This is known as *submersion*.

Sometimes these kids are labeled underachievers, but we don't think of them that way. These kids simply put most of their attention and

energy into their interests and passions, and those often aren't what's being taught at school.

Sometimes gifted people talk about intensities or passions rather than interests. What's the difference?

Passions are things you can't live without and interests are things you like but you can live without.
Boy, 7, California

Interests are so much milder. Passions are all-consuming, like my music. I could not survive without my music.
Girl, 8, New Mexico

A passion is something that rules your life. You want to know everything there is to know and you want to be the best at it. An interest is something that is cool, and you would like to know more, but if you don't that's okay too.
Boy, 8, Oklahoma

I can talk about my interests with friends and others. Never my passions, though. Kids would think I'm weird.
Boy, 9, Idaho

The differences are that I look so deeply into things I am passionate about. Some people are interested in things, but they are not as crazy as I am.
Girl, 10, Ohio

I like learning just for the sake of learning and am interested in many topics, but I have only a few passions. Those are all-consuming. I can work for hours straight on things I enjoy. Those hours become days, then weeks, and before I realize it, I've been working years on the same type of activities I was doing as a 5-year-old. I become so involved in these activities/projects that I lose all track of time.
Boy, 10, Illinois

> "A passion is something that rules your life."

Interests are things that you have a mild interest in. Passions are when you want to know every single little detail about something.
Boy, 10, Colorado

A passion means that something goes deeper in us. It is something that begins to define who we are.
Girl, 11, Michigan

Passion is when you really feel for something. If you have an interest you may just like the topic. Passion is higher than interest, but both can turn into the other.
Girl, 11, Massachusetts

I think you can talk about your interests with people so they get to know you. Passions, though, are out-of-bounds thinking that you shouldn't share unless with a dear friend that really knows you well.
Girl, 11, Kentucky

I think a passion is something you were born to do and an interest is something you like to do.
Boy, 12, New York

Passions are things you think about constantly, you want to know all about them with all your heart and soul. You know you are talking about somebody's passion when you see a "special light in their eye."
Girl, 12, Ohio

Reflection Connection

Do any of these explanations of interests and passions match your own understanding? What is the difference to you?

Make a two-column list. In one column list your interests, in the other your passions. How did you decide what went in one column and what went in the other?

Do you have any hobbies, interests, or passions that others consider unusual?

Completing a 1,000-piece puzzle of the Statue of Liberty made out of words of the Constitution, completing all of the Harry Potter Lego sets, teaching myself algebra for fun, and licking forensic science.
Girl, 9, Pennsylvania

I like to write songs and bird watch.
Boy, 10, Michigan

I have tons! The weirdest ones I have are philosophy and self-improvement. I love thinking about all the possibilities for my life and about why I am here today.
Girl, 12, Maryland

I like to do triathlons, swim team, and karate. I also do softball and cheerleading.
Girl, 12, Indiana

I like to read and many kids call me a nerd but I ignore them because my hobby will be helpful all through life.
Boy, 12, Ohio

A Kid Like You: Zoe, Age 4 ½

Zoe lives with her mom, dad, and cats in a city near Los Angeles, California. Zoe likes where she lives because, she says, "We can walk to the grocery store and the library and the park." She also likes to visit her grandmother, who lives in Los Angeles, and going to museums and basketball games there. And Zoe *loves* to see musicals.

Zoe's love of musicals is more than a passing interest. She developed a passion for musicals early in life. "I have lots of musicals on CD and like to see them onstage to know what the actors are doing when singing," Zoe says. "My favorites are *Les*

⟶

Misérables and *Wicked*. I am learning the piano so I can learn to write my own music."

She also is learning to sing. "I am amazed with Zoe's 'old soul,'" says Miss Jessica, Zoe's voice teacher. "I don't know many people who know so much about musicals!"

Like many parents, Zoe's didn't realize she was different until she started socializing with other kids her age. It just didn't seem to work. Zoe was interested in performing and detailed actions; other 2- and 3-year-olds had very short attention spans, which frustrated Zoe.

When she was 3 years old, she found older kids who shared her interests when she took an acting class. Still, the class's pace did not meet her needs. "I was invited to do a show in my drama class. It was for kids older than me, but the teacher wanted me to do it. I really paid attention and practiced my monologue and dialogue. But the other kids didn't learn theirs so I had to wait for them. It took a really long time." Three months, according to Zoe's mom!

This experience didn't dampen Zoe's enthusiasm for theater, though. "This year I am going to be in a musical theater group with kids who are 7 to 14 years old. I can learn fast and finally get to a place where others speed along too."

For now, Zoe's passion consumes much of her time. But when she thinks about the future she has more plans. "I look forward to going to college someday. I think I will really like it because then I can learn to be a doctor. But I can be an actress now."

Are you a creative person? Explain.

Yes, I like to do art projects and draw. I like to be creative in making Lego structures and using other construction toys.

Boy, 7, Connecticut

I will do anything I can possibly do. When I was 2, I was literally drawing figures that practically looked like the true thing!
Boy, 9, Idaho

I can write good stories. I'm not a good artist so I can think up really, really cool looking pictures in my head but I can't put them down on paper. I can think up really good ideas about just about everything.
Boy, 10, Texas

I really like to be artistically different. I want to stand out from everyone else in all ways.
Girl, 11, Ohio

I believe I'm creative. That is why I was entered in the gifted program. I can make detailed and elaborate stories. I also have an expanded vocabulary. I can also make poems easily since I have such a big vocabulary.
Boy, 11, Texas

Am I creative? No. And I lack the capacity to explain.
Boy, 11, Virginia

Yes, I write, read, and daydream constantly.
Boy, 11, Tennessee

My mind has no limits sometimes. My brain and I get a little bit carried away!
Girl, 11, Pennsylvania

Oh, that's me! I like to create stuff about the ocean and marine mammals because that is what I like the best. I create stuff that has to do with what I'm learning in school.
Girl, 12, Idaho

If I am allowed to do whatever I want I can be creative. But, if I have boundaries and guidelines, I have a difficult time thinking something up because I don't feel like I'm allowed to do whatever I want so I end up doing something completely boring.
Girl, 12, Ohio

I draw when I can, I read almost nonstop. And I daydream sometimes even when I shouldn't.
Boy, 12, Maine

Do you think being creative can get in the way in school? Explain.

Sometimes the other kids don't want to play with me because they say I am bossy. I don't understand why they won't call me by my make-believe name or play the games that I make up sometimes.
Boy, 5, Florida

Yes, because if you get too creative you get carried away and don't do the work you're supposed to and you get bad grades.
Boy, 9, Iowa

No, because being creative is something that makes you *you* and being creative sometimes helps you get extra points on schoolwork.
Girl, 10, Nebraska

NO! Never. If you are creative you will be able to write great stories, find special ways to do math problems, and a lot of other things.
Girl, 10, Iowa

No, because I'm only creative in my TAG class.
Girl, 10, Illinois

Yes, teachers don't like your smart-aleck responses or creative answers on tests.
Boy, 11, Tennessee

Yes, sometimes. Thinking logically is what you need to do to survive schoolwork.

Girl, 11, Ohio

Yeah, I do think that it can get in the way by the fact that if you're creative, you might think too deep into things. Like a simple problem could become really difficult because you might start to analyze it from too many perspectives. Maybe I'm wrong, but maybe I have a point there too.

Girl, 12, Ohio

You always have to follow the rules. Heaven help you if you get creative and it's not part of your adequate preparation for the test.

Boy, 12, Maine

Creativity can be described in many different ways. How do you define creativity? Using that definition, are you creative? How?

There also are many ways to *be* creative—for example through music, art, writing, storytelling, dancing, acting, inventing, graphic design, sciences, martial arts or yoga, and any number of other ways. In what ways are you creative? Are you interested in finding other ways to be creative? What are they? Why?

If you could change anything about your life, what would you change?

Popularity. Just because I'm gifted, people think I'm a nerd.

Boy, 11, Ohio

I think I would change the fact that I am a shy person and am hard on myself most of the time.

Boy, 11, Ohio

Nothing! If I change one thing it might lead my life in a whole different direction.

Girl, 11, Oklahoma

I would probably try to be nicer to other people. I can get edgy and moody sometimes, and I'm not an angel. I wish that I would give people more slack.

Girl, 11, New Hampshire

How does life (or school) force gifted people to underachieve?

It's kind of hard not to underachieve because all the assignments are things that I already am good at doing.

Girl, 8, Ohio

Sometimes you get tired of always being the smart kid. It makes you want to be like everyone else and underachieve like making low grades on purpose. Sometimes if you are a straight-A student and get no bad grades then other kids will make fun of you and call you a nerd.

Girl, 10, Pennsylvania

Sometimes you know all the answers, and the teacher wants you to let other kids get a chance. I don't answer anymore. Sometimes I don't even hear what is asked. I hear blah, blah, but don't really care because expectations are I'll know the stuff so why bother asking me.

Boy, 11, Indiana

Sometimes I am embarrassed because my teacher recognizes me in front of the class, and all the kids stare at me like I am some freak from outer space. I try my best to let other people have their say, but it is really hard to contain myself in some situations.

Girl, 11, New Hampshire

One word: PRESSURE!

Boy, 11, Georgia

When the teachers give us really easy homework we get totally careless because it is so boring that we miss problems. It makes us look like we can't do hard work, when in fact we would do much better in a challenging context.
Girl, 11, Vancouver, Canada

Sometimes gifted people get loads of pressure from other kids about being smart and they end up underachieving so they can prove they are just like everyone else.
Boy, 12, Oklahoma

SUBMERSION is when someone hides his or her abilities. Do you (or does anyone you know) do this? Why do you (or they) do it?

Yes, I do this. I guess because it's kind of embarrassing to be smarter or different. Now that I've skipped ahead to fourth grade, I might do it less because that's more the pace that I'm learning at.
Girl, 8, Ohio

Yes, a boy I know will retreat and act ashamed about being special. Sometimes he gets depressed for months. It makes me angry, because I wonder if someone has been belittling him.
Girl, 9, Kentucky

Yes, I do because I'm afraid people will laugh at me when I say I take dance classes.
Boy, 9, Minnesota

Yes, I do. This helps me get mind time to think about things I really want to do in school. I sit a good part of the day doing redundant work. So, if I hide inside my mind, I cannot feel so overwhelmingly bored.
Girl, 12, Michigan

I think they are hiding so they can dig and dig into material to learn it at a depth they want to know. If caught, they would have to do what everyone else is doing.
Boy, 12, Wisconsin

They might be doing something they can get very easily, and it's not challenging enough. They might often be bored in the classroom. They might think the class work is too straightforward.
Girl, 12, New Jersey

Underachievement is a good thing so they can imagine and be creative in thinking about interesting topics instead of doing the same old work they do year after year.
Girl, 12, Ohio

Reflection Connection

Why do you think some gifted kids choose submersion? Most adults would probably say that submersion and underachievement are bad ideas for gifted kids because then kids are not learning as much as they could be. Do you agree or disagree? Why? Can submersion or underachievement be a good thing? Why?

Looking Ahead:
Plans and Hopes

For most kids, childhood is a time for playing and having fun, and gifted kids are no different. But many gifted kids also are thinking a lot about the future—their educations and careers, for starters, and "bigger" issues too, like technological innovation, the environment, and world peace.

Many gifted kids are nervous about the future. They fear they won't live up to their potential, or contribute to society in ways that give them satisfaction, or become happy adults. But most gifted kids we know feel hopeful when looking ahead. They look forward to using their abilities to pursue challenging and rewarding goals.

What are your future plans?

I want to be an actress. I love the feeling of be-ing onstage, of the curtain rising on my show.

Girl, 8, Pennsylvania

To become a veterinarian and a dog breeder who shows dogs.

Boy, 9, Massachusetts

Be a professional organizer. I want to help organize homes, offices, and businesses. When my parents move out, I want to buy the house we are living in.

Girl, 9, Ohio

Travel and buy at least seven cats; be an opera singer and live in New York or Paris.

Girl, 9, Illinois

I would like to become an elementary or high school teacher—well, I'll be both—so I can help other kids like me actually LEARN something instead of just memorizing for a test.

Boy, 10, Iowa

I want to be the first girl to ever play for the Ohio State Buckeyes football team. I want to be a quarterback.

Girl, 10, Ohio

To marry my crush and be a millionaire; to practice law, accounting, and to be an entertainer.

Girl, 10, West Virginia

My future goal is to become a scientist and make a cheaper car that is solar powered.

Boy, 10, Texas

I want to go to college and become a ballet dancer, and either a part-time author, artist, or something to do with animals.

Girl, 10, Arkansas

I plan to graduate from high school and then go to college to be a zoologist. From here, I'll make a splash with my own TV show and travel the world discovering new species of animals.
Boy, 11, Ohio

My future plans are to be either a lawyer or a fashion designer . . . maybe both!
Girl, 11, Ohio

My future plans are to go to an awesome university and become a senator, or even PRESIDENT!
Boy, 11, Arizona

I want to become a veterinarian. And, to get people to quit being dumb about families and the environment. Imperial Queen of the Galaxy? Perhaps.
Girl, 11, Oklahoma

I plan to be an engineer or an author. I have been really creative so I could juggle careers and write a book when I get home from my engineering job.
Boy, 11, Texas

I hope to become a major league baseball or basketball player. If I'm not good enough, I'll settle for being a scientist.
Boy, 11, Arkansas

"I want to do something that changes life as we know it."

My future plans are to become a doctor or a veterinarian or become the FIRST FEMALE PRESIDENT.
Girl, 12, Georgia

I don't really have any concrete plans. I just want it to happen as it comes.
Boy, 12, Ohio

I want to be a cook and go to Yale.
Boy, 12, Pennsylvania

Uhhh, future plans? I want to discover or make something great, but I don't want people to know who I am. I don't want to be written down in history books as someone special and worth recognizing. But I want to do something that changes life as we know it.
Girl, 12, Ohio

It's estimated that workers of your generation will change careers at least five times during their lives. If this is true, what five (or more) careers do you think you'll have in your life?

What would you like to learn about that, up until now, you haven't had time to explore?

Rocks and minerals. These might change, but for now my interests lie in the makeup of the earth's crust.
Girl, 8, New Jersey

I'd like to learn about how dogs think!
Girl, 9, Massachusetts

My future plans are to pass over to high school. When I get there, get good grades and get on to college. There I will earn a master's degree and make it into NASA.
Boy, 9, Kentucky

I would like to learn about other gifted kids, because I sometimes think I am the only gifted one in a gifted class!
Girl, 10, Ontario, Canada

EVERYGHING! There are so many things I want to learn about, but we don't have time in school. I see this as a major problem when I have to choose what to do as a career. How will I know what to pick when I don't know much about any of the jobs?
Boy, 10, Michigan

I would really want to learn more about animals because they are so fun and always there for you.
Girl, 11, Ohio

I would like to learn what my parents are thinking when they get mad, sad, glad, or impressed at what I'm doing.
Boy, 11, Texas

I want to go to vet school now. My mom sets the limit at dissecting lizards and frogs—but I would like to see more!
Girl, 11, Texas

More about World War II and the Korean War. I read a 585-page book on World War II outside of my schoolwork.
Boy, 11, Iowa

I've always wanted to learn more about computers. Someday, I want to make my own super-computer with super-high-speed Internet connection and a super-virus protector with a super-firewall. With the super-computer, I'll make my own super-games and test them and put them on the market.
Boy, 11, Iowa

A lot of things such as history, space, and the future. I want to learn things that teachers don't teach about, things that I would have to go someplace and figure out for myself. This is challenging, and fun too.
Girl, 12, Ohio

I would like to learn more about mythology. I enjoy learning about the beliefs and fears of ancient people.

Boy, 12, Iowa

I would like to learn about three things: space, space travel and black holes, and other forms of life. I'd also like to learn about time travel. And lastly, I really want to learn about religions. I don't really have a religion right now, because there are so many options.

Girl, 12, Ohio

Probably about why people made things the way they did. Like why is the alphabet in that order?

Girl, 12, Ohio

Reflection Connection

When talking about their hopes and plans for the future, kids often say they'd like to be a doctor, lawyer, veterinarian, or another well-known job. If you want to find out about some less common careers, take a look through a resource you probably have at home: the Yellow Pages. Begin by flipping through the book, looking for headings that sound interesting (like "liquidator" or "mud jacking contractor"). Some headings will be actual occupations (like "pawn broker") and others will be more general (like "robots" and "youth organizations"). You may have to do some research to find out what jobs are associated with the general headings.

Next, pick one or two occupations and do some research to learn about them. If you find something really interesting, share it with your teacher. Maybe you can get a person who does that job to visit your class and talk about it, or maybe you can set up a field trip to someone's place of work.

Think about the future. Describe how you think school will be for you until graduation day.

I think that I am going to be the smartest person in college (if Joey does not go to the same college).

Girl, 9, Iowa

I think things will continue to be easy for me. I might not be as bored in class, though. There will probably be a thing or two that will be difficult for me, but I am ready.

Boy, 10, Texas

I think school will just get easier and easier until I go to college. But I hope in the future that each grade would get more challenging and interesting. Is this wishful thinking?

Girl, 11, Texas

I will be learning new things in some classes and be really bored in others. I think I will be advanced in most every class except band and choir. I probably won't be the most athletic person ever.

Girl, 12, Idaho

I think I'll probably excel in all my classes. I'll probably have people coming up to me and begging me for answers.

Boy, 12, Wisconsin

I think my future will be good because I have a good head on my shoulders and I know what I'm doing, so when problems arise I can work through them. I can't wait to find out what my future holds. It's gonna be great—you'll see.

Boy, 12, Ohio

Imagine you are 50 years old. Reflect back on your life's accomplishments.

I graduated early and went to college and grad school. I won lots of dog shows and cared for many animals as a vet.
Girl, 9, Massachusetts

I look back and think how smart I was when I was young. What happened when I grew up?!
Girl, 10, Iowa

I'm a Hall of Fame inductee in the NFL and am still working as an engineer.
Boy, 11, Texas

I remember all my famous movies, and watch them while saying the words right out loud. I also remember my Grammys and all my adoring fans. And if I'm not an actress, then I'll remember all the kids that I reached out and touched while I was teaching and I will always remember their smiling faces!
Girl, 11, Washington

I graduated from Harvard. As a 35-year-old, I started a car company. During my first term as a senator, I ran for president when I was 37 years old. I was elected for two terms and here I am today!
Boy, 11, Alabama

I figure I am the type of person who does what I want and never stopped for roadblocks. I found ways to hop right over them.
Girl, 11, Texas

My job is to tell my grandchildren about my accomplishments and help them get good opportunities in school.
Boy, 12, Oklahoma

I've been a great vet and written a couple books about my career.
Boy, 12, Wisconsin

Reflection Connection

Potential.

This is a word gifted kids hear a lot. For many, hearing what others think about their *potential* can leave them feeling a little nervous. If that sounds like you, take a look at what one former gifted kid—now a gifted adult—has to say about the pressure of potential. KaSandra, age 19, has been through the same thing.

"I was often told that I could do or be anything I wanted because I was so smart. But I had a hard time figuring out what this really meant. It ended up meaning to me that if I didn't get all A's, act sweet and agreeable all the time, and have loads of friends, I was letting my family down. It took quite a while for me to overcome the stigma of potential in my life."

But KaSandra did get over the worries that came from potential and expectations and learned to make decisions for herself. "You cannot let other people's expectations decide for you what you should do," she says. "You need to use your emotions along with your intellect to help guide you toward a career destination."

Does having potential leave you feeling a little nervous? Why or why not?

If you could change anything about the world, what would it be?

I would like there to be more animals and less pollution.
Boy, 8, California

I would try to stop pollution and the cutting down of trees, and help endangered animals. I want to spread the word or organize something, but I feel too shy.
Girl, 8, Pennsylvania

War.
Girl, 9, Wisconsin

I think I would change
the fact that people
are exclusive and
sometimes mean
to people who are
different.
Boy, 11, Ohio

> "Everyone would go to bed safely and wake up in the morning and think, 'Another beautiful day, I'm thankful to be alive.'"

No more violence or diseases.
Boy, 11, Ohio

Stop world hunger!
Girl, 11, Oklahoma

I would force scientific developments like renewable energies.
Boy, 11, Germany

If I could change something about the world, everyone would have
a nice house to live in, food to eat, nice clothes to wear, and a large
loving family who was there for them when they needed it. There
wouldn't be wars, and peace and justice would rule the earth. Everyone
would go to bed safely and wake up in the morning and think,
"Another beautiful day, I'm thankful to be alive." If we lived in that
kind of world, to me, it would be perfect. We need problems, but not
ones that families have to fret about for days, weeks, months, years
on end.
Girl, 11, New Hampshire

If I could change anything else, it would be all the HATE in the world.
I can't solve world problems, but I pray for those who don't understand
that we try to help EVERYONE as much as we possibly can.
Girl, 12, Ohio

A Kid Like You: Callie, Age 12

C allie lives in Ohio with her sister and parents. "I have no 'real' pets," she says, "but I do have one on Neopets.com." Callie has a large extended family in Bangladesh, where she has visited once and hopes to visit again soon.

Callie enjoys imagining what she might do when she gets older and where she might end up. "The future is a place I live in every now and then," she says. "The future is where possibilities wait for me. It's different from the past. The past is where the 'been there, done that' of life tries to rope in my spirit. I say follow your dreams. Try new things and see what happens."

Callie feels both hopeful and nervous about the future, and she believes a lot of gifted kids feel the same way.

"The future can be a scary place for a kid with lots of potential," she says. "I remember people (mostly family) being really excited when I was first identified [as gifted]. Everyone seemed to be so full of expectations that I'd be some sort of surgeon, attorney, or even the President! This was a lot of pressure on me. I didn't want to let anyone down, so I took the safe route with my work. I did *exactly* what teachers said to the letter. I earned straight A's on everything since I knew that was what was expected."

But after a while, doing what was expected began to grind on Callie. "I became very angry and didn't like anything about my work or myself. I lost a lot of the energy I had about learning. I was doing what I was told to do. Jump this high, write this much, score this well. This was my life and I hated it.

"When you are a smart kid, all the people around you expect more out of you. Over time you start to expect more out of you too. And this feeling never leaves. You drive yourself nuts trying to do more and more and you lose the time for yourself."

Callie describes the pressure of expectations and potential this way: "It's sort of like field mice. They have to be on edge

⟶

to survive predators. This is how I see gifted kids acting. We flit around from idea to idea trying things on for size but have to always be worried about something bigger than us breathing down our necks."

This may sound like a pretty negative view of life, but Callie doesn't think it's all negative. In fact, she's hopeful about what lies ahead. "We (gifted kids) do have a very positive way of seeing the future," she says. "I am a hopeful person and this keeps me thinking good thoughts. My hope is to keep looking ahead instead of behind. Hope for the future is always a positive thing. It lets you loose from expectations. It helps you imagine what interests are yet to be found out."

Callie probably spends a lot more time thinking about the future than most kids. "My mom says I'm too flighty," she admits. But Callie has some pretty smart thoughts about the present too.

"People are moving too fast in the world," she says. "No one seems to take time to daydream or do nothing anymore. And when I do, I get told to do something more productive. Sometimes I don't want to be productive. I just want to take some time off for nothing. I think this would be a good thing for everyone to do. It helps me feel less nervous and stressed. I think it would help everyone."

Do you feel hopeful about the future? Explain.

I do. I have had success in the past and am sure this will blossom in the future.
Girl, 8, Pennsylvania

Not really, because the world might become too polluted for life.
Boy, 10, New Mexico

No, because realistically my goals are about 35 percent reachable considering that you can only control so much of the future.
Girl, 10, Virginia

Yes. Certain medical procedures are
painful and I hope technology
will invent something less
painful. Just things like
that, improvement in things.
Peace!!!!!!!
Girl, 11, Michigan

> "I hope to have
> a really good life
> because of my
> abilities."

Yes, but I will have to get a little
organized.
Boy, 11, Louisiana

I think the world is going to get a lot worse. People just don't care
about people anymore—it is all about money—and the music of my
generation is not very inspirational.
Girl, 11, Alabama

I cannot say that I feel hopeful about my future. My family does not
have much money to send me to college.
Boy, 12, Iowa

Yes, I do because I hope to have a really good life because
of my abilities.
Girl, 12, Wisconsin

Yes! I have faith in myself and I always will!
Boy, 12, Vermont

Reflection Connection

Many kids in this chapter express high ideals and passionate
hopes for making the world a better place. What are your
ideals and hopes? What can you do to inspire such passionate
hopefulness in others?

A Final Word

This book is a kind of conversation between you and the hundreds of gifted kids in these pages about the struggles and rewards of giftedness. Although we've reached the end of this conversation, our hope is that you will keep the discussion going. When you feel pressured, abnormal, lonely, or stressed out, or when you want to share your passions or hopes, talk with someone. You can talk with parents, guardians, teachers, or other kids. Better yet, find gifted adults or older peers who have lived through the situations you face and invite them to discuss their experiences.

Some of the most important things to remember about being gifted are that you're not weird, you're not alone, and you can have fun! Just remember that your potential is *your* potential. Try not to let the pressure from others get you down.

We were pleased when a kid like you—Lisa, 10 years old—summed up our point.

"Do what feels right to you," Lisa said. "If you like to read—read. If you like math, do it. If you are dramatic, play hard." She went on: "I won't spend a lot of time waiting for something good to happen. I'm making it happen. You can too!"

We couldn't have said it better ourselves!

About the Authors

Robert A. Schultz, Ph.D., spends the majority of his life helping raise his children. He spends "spare" time as an associate professor of gifted education and curriculum studies at the University of Toledo (Ohio). A man of many hats, Bob coordinates the university's Middle Grades Teacher Education program; travels the country as a consultant in Gifted Education and Curriculum Development/Evaluation; teaches in public schools; researches and writes about giftedness; and, most importantly to his kids, is a hockey coach.

Bob and his wife, Cindy, live in Toledo, Ohio, but eventually they will retire and while away their time sailing in the Caribbean. Until then, Bob plans to continue helping parents, kids, teachers, and schools meet the diverse needs of gifted learners in and out of classrooms.

James R. Delisle, Ph.D., is distinguished professor of education at Kent State University in Ohio, where he directs the undergraduate and graduate programs in gifted child education. He is a former classroom teacher, special education teacher, and teacher of gifted children (and still teaches gifted seventh- and eighth-graders one day a week). He has received several teaching honors, including Kent State University's most prestigious distinction, the Distinguished Teaching Award, in 2004. However, the most important award came recently when one of his former fourth-grade students selected him, upon high school graduation, as his "Most Inspirational Teacher." Jim also has served as a counselor for gifted adolescents and their families. He is the author or coauthor of more than 200 articles and 14 books, including the best-selling *Gifted Kids' Survival Guide: A Teen Handbook* and *When Gifted Kids Don't Have All the Answers: How to Meet Their Social and Emotional Needs* (both with Judy Galbraith).

Jim and his wife, Deb, live in Kent, Ohio, most of the year and in North Myrtle Beach, South Carolina, when school is out.

Bob and Jim also are the coauthors of *More Than a Test Score: What Teens Say About Being Gifted, Talented, or Otherwise Extra-Ordinary.*

Other Great Books from Free Spirit

More Than a Test Score
Teens Talk About Being Gifted, Talented,
or Otherwise Extra-Ordinary
by Robert A. Schultz, Ph.D. and Jim Delisle, Ph.D.
We often hear about gifted kids, but seldom
from them. Drawing on the voices of thousands
of gifted teenagers from around the world, this
book is a real-life look at what being gifted
means to teens today. Essential reading for
gifted teens and the adults who care about
them. For ages 13 & up,
$14.95; 176 pp.; softcover; illus.; 6" x 9"

The Gifted Kids' Survival Guide
For Ages 10 & Under
Revised & Updated Edition
by Judy Galbraith, M.A.
First published in 1984, newly revised and
updated, this book has helped countless young
gifted children realize they're not alone, they're
not "weird," and being smart, talented, and creative is a bonus, not a burden. Includes advice
from hundreds of gifted kids. For ages 10 &
under.
$9.95; 104 pp.; softcover; illus.; 6" x 9"

The Gifted Kids' Survival Guide
A Teen Handbook
Revised, Expanded, and Updated Edition
by Judy Galbraith, M.A., and Jim Delisle, Ph.D.
Vital information on giftedness, IQ, school success, college planning, stress, perfectionism,
and much more. For ages 11–18.
$15.95; 304 pp.; softcover; illus.; 7¹/₄" x 9¹/₄"

Speak Up and Get Along!
Tools to Make Friends, Stop Teasing, and Feel
Good About Yourself
by Scott Cooper
A handy toolbox of ways to get along with others.
Twenty-one concrete strategies kids can pull out and
use to express themselves, build relationships, end
arguments and fights, halt bullying, and beat unhappy
feelings. For ages 8–12.
$12.95; 128 pp.; softcover; illus.; 6" x 9"

Stress Can Really Get on Your NERVES!
by Trevor Romain and Elizabeth Verdick
More kids than ever feel worried, stressed out, and
anxious every day. This book is a helping hand for those
kids. Reassuring words, silly jokes, and light-hearted
cartoons let them know they're not the only worry-warts
on the planet—and they can learn to manage their
stress. For ages 8–13.
$9.95; 96 pp.; softcover; illus.; 5¹⁄₈" x 7"

Perfectionism
What's Bad About Being Too Good?
Revised and Updated Edition
by Miriam Adderholdt, Ph.D., and Jan Goldberg
This revised and updated edition includes new research
and statistics on the causes and consequences of perfectionism, biographical sketches of famous perfectionists
and risk takers, and resources for readers who want to
know more. For ages 13 & up.
$12.95; 136 pp.; softcover; illus.; 6" x 9"

The Survival Guide for Kids with LD*
*(Learning Differences)
Revised & Updated Edition
by Gary Fisher, Ph.D., and Rhoda Cummings, Ed.D.
Kids need to know they're smart and can learn, they
just might learn differently. This book explains to kids
what LD means (and doesn't mean); helps them deal
with their feelings; suggests ways to get along better in
school and at home; and inspires them to set goals and
plan for the future. For ages 8 & up.
$10.95; 112 pp.; softcover; illus.; 6" x 9"